Aboriginal Cultures in Alberta

Five Hundred Generations

Susan Berry and Jack Brink

Aboriginal Advisory	Reg Crowshoe, Peter Ladouceur, Rita Marten and Russell Willier
Supported by	Syncrude Canada
Written by	Susan Berry and Jack Brink
Project Managers	Hannah Aaron and Steve Fisher
Edited by	Sylvia Vance
Photography	Brad Callihoo, New Visions Photography
Design	Carolyn Lilgert
Published	Copyright 2004 by The Provincial Museum of Alberta

Library and Archives Canada Cataloguing in Publication

Berry, Susan
 Aboriginal cultures in Alberta : five hundred generations / Susan Berry and Jack Brink.

ISBN 0-7785-2852-9

  1. Indians of North America—Alberta—History.
  2. Métis—Alberta—History.
  3. Alberta—Anthropology.
  4. Prehistoric Archaeology—Alberta.

I. Brink, Jack II. The Provincial Museum of Alberta III. Title.

E78.A34B48 2004 971.23004'97
C2004-095553-4

Printed on	Centura Silk
Printed and bound in Canada by	McCallum Printing Group Inc. Edmonton

Alberta

Contents

Introduction

Syncrude is honoured to have played an instrumental role in the development of the Provincial Museum's Syncrude Gallery of Aboriginal Culture. Now we celebrate the publication of this comprehensive book, *Aboriginal Cultures in Alberta: Five Hundred Generations.*

Since its beginnings, Syncrude has been a Canadian leader in developing strong relationships with Aboriginal communities. Our company is one of the largest employers of Aboriginal people in Canada, and we are committed to furthering the participation of Aboriginal people in Canadian society.

In the same spirit, Syncrude is proud to sponsor this beautiful book, which will enhance the experience of visitors to the Gallery. In these pages, you will find striking images of Alberta's rich and diverse past, as well as clear proof of the vibrancy of contemporary Aboriginal culture. The stories told here help us remember a vital part of Canada's history and help us appreciate the contributions Aboriginal people continue to make to Canadian society.

I acknowledge the former Director of the Provincial Museum of Alberta, the late Dr. Philip Stepney, and the present Director, Dr. Bruce McGillivray, for their commitment to telling the historical and contemporary stories of Aboriginal people through the Syncrude Gallery of Aboriginal Culture. The Gallery continues to evolve, and I congratulate the entire staff of the Provincial Museum of Alberta for publishing this impressive book and for their ongoing work to create one of Canada's finest galleries of Aboriginal history and culture.

James E. Carter
President and Chief Operating Officer
Syncrude Canada Ltd.

Director's Message

Aboriginal history in Alberta is a story of great richness, diversity and depth. Doing justice to the story in a 10,000 square-foot gallery was one of the most challenging projects ever undertaken by the Provincial Museum of Alberta. The success of the gallery depended upon the collaborative efforts of a wide range of talented people. While not all of these individuals were involved in the subsequent production of *Aboriginal Cultures in Alberta: Five Hundred Generations*, their contributions inform every page.

Foremost among our valued partners is the Museum's Aboriginal Advisory Committee. Reg Crowshoe, Peter Ladouceur, Rita Marten and Russell Willier supplied both the overarching vision for the Gallery and the guiding hand needed to make that vision a reality. We were also greatly assisted by Elders from twenty-two First Nations and Métis communities who visited the Gallery while work was underway and offered their insights and advice. Aboriginal residents throughout the province graciously participated in interviews conducted with Museum staff. Consultants, both Aboriginal and non-Aboriginal, contributed their expertise to every aspect of the project, from curatorial research and graphic design to multi-media production and educational programming.

None of this would have been possible without Syncrude Canada's generous support. Long recognized as one of Canada's most community-minded corporate leaders, Syncrude made it possible for the Syncrude Gallery to attain a level of excellence of which I am very proud. But Syncrude's commitment to the project did not end when the Gallery opened. Syncrude also funded a Gallery interpreter, co-sponsors our Aboriginal Internship Program in Museum Practices in partnership with the National Aboriginal Achievement Foundation, and financed the publication of *Aboriginal Cultures in Alberta: Five Hundred Generations*. I extend to Syncrude and its leadership my deep gratitude for their long-term commitment to this project.

If the Syncrude Gallery of Aboriginal Culture was one of our Museum's most challenging projects, it has also been one of our most rewarding. The positive reviews that the Gallery has received since it opened in the fall of 1997, the steady rate of visitors and the expressions of support from Aboriginal and non-Aboriginal commentators testify to its effectiveness as an educational and cultural resource. I hope that *Aboriginal Cultures in Alberta: Five Hundred Generations* will help expand the success of the Gallery beyond the walls of the Provincial Museum.

W. Bruce McGillivray
Director, Provincial Museum of Alberta

Acknowledgements

I would like to extend special thanks to members of the Archaeological Survey, past and present, who contributed greatly to the work presented in the Syncrude Gallery of Aboriginal Culture. A team of determined and talented people worked on this project from start to finish—contributing ideas for the displays, the storyline, artifact suggestions and the text. It is a measure of the success of this team that the line between who contributed what is now forever blurred, lost in the presentation of a single story throughout the Gallery and in this book.

Although I no longer know who wrote what, certainly much of the text in the Archaeology section of this guide book is the product of their labour. Collectively we worked and collectively I thank them: Alwynne Beaudoin, Bob Dawe, Jack Ives, David Link, Heinz Pyszczyk, Brian Ronaghan, Rod Vickers and Milt Wright. Trevor Peck was brought in on contract to specifically help with the archaeological portion of the Gallery. Over several years he did yeoman's work: conducting library research, chasing down artifacts and photographs, contributing ideas and valuable discussion. I thank Trevor for his help and dedication.

Karen Giering likewise provided me with much help in organizing the text, photographs and other images used in this guide. I would also like to thank the Aboriginal Advisory Committee for their support and guidance in shaping the content of the archaeology section of the Gallery. Finally I would like to extend my personal thanks to the late Dr. Phillip Stepney. He was determined to bring a new gallery of Aboriginal history and culture to the Provincial Museum of Alberta, and he fought to make that dream come true.

Jack Brink
Curator of Archaeology

Just as the Syncrude Gallery of Aboriginal Culture was built through the collaborative efforts of many people, so too was this book. Collaboration began with the Museum's Aboriginal Advisory Committee, whose good counsel laid the foundation for all our work. For their insights, guidance and support, my heartfelt thanks to Committee members Reg Crowshoe, Peter Ladouceur, Rita Marten and Russell Willier.

Special thanks go to those individuals who worked with Ethnology staff on particular Gallery topics. Allan Pard, Jerry Potts, Irvine Scalplock and Herman Yellow Old Woman gave generously of their time and expertise to educate me about Blackfoot culture and to assist with the development of related displays. James Ahnassay, Sidney Fineday, Raven Makkanaw, the late Gordon Rain and Frank Weaselhead guided discussions of spiritual life, identifying key messages and assisting with artifact selection. The late Delia Gray provided valued advice on Métis history.

A number of Ethnology staff members past and present also contributed to this effort. Peter Crossen and Gail Duiker conducted extensive archival research. Rhonda DeLorme, Linda Lewis and Audrey Yardley-Jones travelled across Alberta recording interviews with local residents. Audrey also compiled the graphics images and secured permission for their use. Ruth McConnell contributed several texts on spiritual life and life in the north, while Rhonda DeLorme and the late Dorothy Daniels wrote original drafts for much of the contemporary section.

Very special thanks go to the many First Nations and Métis individuals who generously shared their knowledge, perspectives and personal experiences with Museum staff. Their contributions enriched *Aboriginal Cultures in Alberta* immeasurably and made working on this project a privilege and a joy.

Susan Berry
Curator of Ethnology

Above:
At the end of the Ice Age many exotic plants and animals appeared on the Alberta landscape.

Right:
Ice-free corridor between the British Columbian and Continental glaciers around 12,000 years ago.

The End of the Ice Age

Around 18,000 years ago Alberta was covered by an enormous sheet of ice that had its centre about where Hudson Bay is now. Animal populations were located northwest and south of the province. These species included mammoth, camel, bison, horse and bighorn sheep and predators like lions and short-faced bears. As the climate warmed, ice gradually receded from the province. Water from the melting ice sheets carved out deep valleys.

At the end of the Ice Age about 12,000 years ago new landscapes were available and animals spread into Alberta both from the north and the south. During this period mammoths and other animals went extinct, although bison survived and evolved into a new species. Caribou receded to the north and wapiti (elk) spread across the continent from the north.

How and when the first Aboriginal people came to the New World remains uncertain. But clear proof of human occupation exists in the Northern Yukon 18,000 years ago. Human occupation of Alberta, however, had to wait until the ice sheet had melted sufficiently so that plants and animals could colonize the landscape.

As melting began, an ice-free corridor opened between the glaciers that covered most of British Columbia and the massive Continental glacier that was centred on Hudson Bay. This gap between the glaciers first opened along the eastern foothills of the Rocky Mountains and may have been the route by which the Americas were first populated. If so, some of the earliest archaeological sites in the New World may be discovered in Alberta. Indeed, the oldest archaeological sites located so far in Alberta do occur along the Eastern Slopes.

However, it is also possible that the earliest people to cross the Bering Land Bridge moved south along the Pacific coastline.

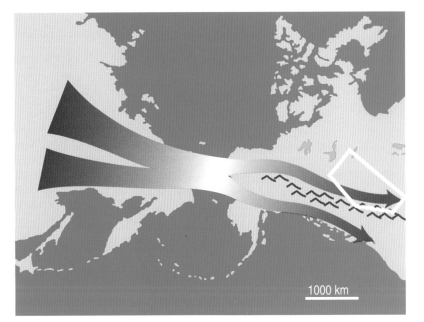

1000 km

Travel along the coast could have been easier at this time because the water contained in the massive glaciers resulted in lower sea levels, thereby exposing more land along the coast.

The exact timing and route of travel are much debated, but Aboriginal populations have been living in Alberta for at least 12,000 years. Elsewhere in the New World, there are tantalizing suggestions that people may have been here for much longer, perhaps even arriving before the last great glaciation.

Above:
The first Aboriginal groups in the New World could have moved south along the Pacific coast or across the interior along the east side of the Rocky Mountains.

Right:
The Vermilion Lakes region of Banff National Park. Courtesy Parks Canada.

Below:
Excavations at Vermilion Lakes site near Banff. Courtesy Parks Canada.

Below:
This Clovis point from Thorsby is about 11,000 years old.

Bottom:
Folsom point from Grande Prairie. Age 10,500 years old.

How Old Is the Past?

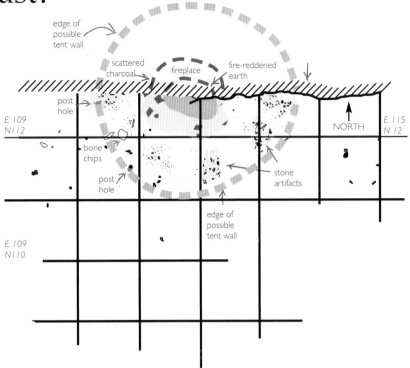

The oldest archaeological sites discovered in Alberta date between 9000 and 11,000 years ago and include sites called Vermilion Lakes, James Pass and Sibbald Creek, all located in Alberta's eastern slopes. These sites contain durable stone tools and the bones of animals as well as the remains of camp activities such as fireplaces. The earliest people hunted big game animals including bison. They also must have consumed a wide variety of small animals and edible plants. Although we know they had the use of fire, we know almost nothing about their dwellings or clothing. A rare exception was found at Vermilion Lakes near Banff, where a circular arrangement of artifacts suggests people there were living in a shelter. Dated at more than 10,000 years old, these are the remains of the oldest shelter known in Canada.

Now all that is left of the multitude of tools these early people used are those made of stone. We have found the knives and scrapers but not the handles that held them. There are spearheads but no spears. We know very little about the people themselves, since their physical remains have not yet been found and other aspects of their culture have not been preserved.

The oldest known types of artifacts in Alberta are Clovis and Folsom spear points. These are called fluted points because of a characteristic channel or flute on each side near the base, which allowed the points to be tied securely to the foreshaft of a spear.

Fluted points have been recovered from excavations at James Pass west of Sundre and Sibbald Creek west of Calgary.

The earliest Aboriginal people in Alberta were in contact with other groups over a wide region of the continent. Even 10,000 years ago, people shared similar styles of artifacts with distant people and used stone obtained through trade from hundreds of kilometres away. Some Alberta points, for example, are made of Knife River Flint, a type of stone that is only found in North Dakota, some 1000 kilometres away.

Above:
A sketch of an excavation at the Vermilion Lakes site showing a circular arrangement of artifacts. Dated at more than 10,000 years, this site is the oldest shelter known in Canada.

Above Left:
Excavations at Sibbald Creek site.

Above:
Bases of spear points from Sibbald Creek site. Age 9000-10,000 years old.

Ancient Tools from the Past

Points in Time

The spear is the oldest type of weapon used in Alberta. It was primarily used from about 11,000 to 8000 years ago, but some spears were used in recent times. A powerful weapon, the spear required close contact with wild game animals and put hunters at considerable risk. Some spears could have been made from a single shaft with a stone tip tied to one end. Others were more complex tools that included a detachable foreshaft, which allowed rapid reloading. Whether thrust by hand or thrown a short distance, spears were a close-range weapon that delivered a great deal of force to the target.

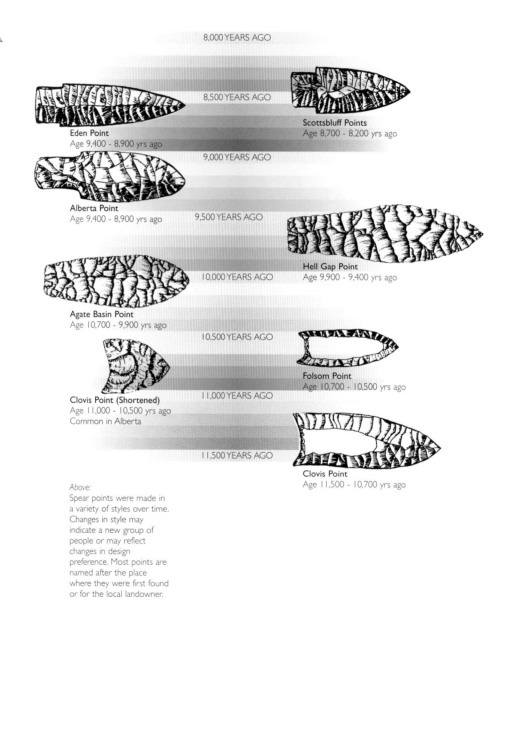

8,000 YEARS AGO

8,500 YEARS AGO

Eden Point
Age 9,400 - 8,900 yrs ago

Scottsbluff Points
Age 8,700 - 8,200 yrs ago

9,000 YEARS AGO

Alberta Point
Age 9,400 - 8,900 yrs ago

9,500 YEARS AGO

Hell Gap Point
Age 9,900 - 9,400 yrs ago

10,000 YEARS AGO

Agate Basin Point
Age 10,700 - 9,900 yrs ago

10,500 YEARS AGO

Folsom Point
Age 10,700 - 10,500 yrs ago

Clovis Point (Shortened)
Age 11,000 - 10,500 yrs ago
Common in Alberta

11,000 YEARS AGO

11,500 YEARS AGO

Clovis Point
Age 11,500 - 10,700 yrs ago

Above:
Spear points were made in a variety of styles over time. Changes in style may indicate a new group of people or may reflect changes in design preference. Most points are named after the place where they were first found or for the local landowner.

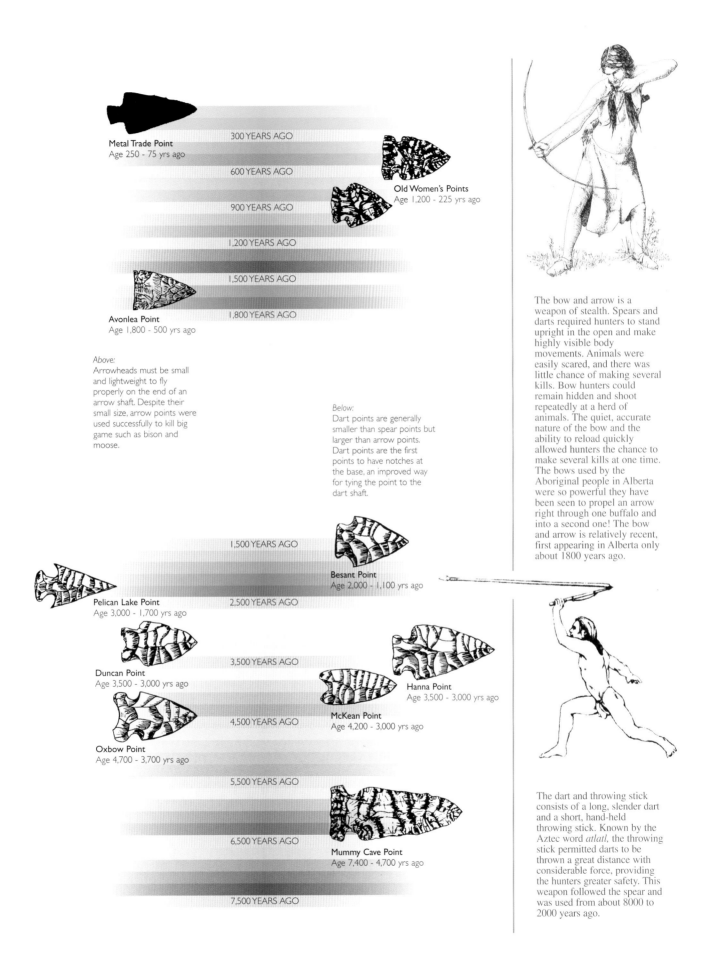

Metal Trade Point
Age 250 - 75 yrs ago

300 YEARS AGO

600 YEARS AGO

Old Women's Points
Age 1,200 - 225 yrs ago

900 YEARS AGO

1,200 YEARS AGO

1,500 YEARS AGO

Avonlea Point
Age 1,800 - 500 yrs ago

1,800 YEARS AGO

Above:
Arrowheads must be small and lightweight to fly properly on the end of an arrow shaft. Despite their small size, arrow points were used successfully to kill big game such as bison and moose.

Below:
Dart points are generally smaller than spear points but larger than arrow points. Dart points are the first points to have notches at the base, an improved way for tying the point to the dart shaft.

1,500 YEARS AGO

Besant Point
Age 2,000 - 1,100 yrs ago

Pelican Lake Point
Age 3,000 - 1,700 yrs ago

2,500 YEARS AGO

Duncan Point
Age 3,500 - 3,000 yrs ago

3,500 YEARS AGO

Hanna Point
Age 3,500 - 3,000 yrs ago

McKean Point
Age 4,200 - 3,000 yrs ago

4,500 YEARS AGO

Oxbow Point
Age 4,700 - 3,700 yrs ago

5,500 YEARS AGO

Mummy Cave Point
Age 7,400 - 4,700 yrs ago

6,500 YEARS AGO

7,500 YEARS AGO

The bow and arrow is a weapon of stealth. Spears and darts required hunters to stand upright in the open and make highly visible body movements. Animals were easily scared, and there was little chance of making several kills. Bow hunters could remain hidden and shoot repeatedly at a herd of animals. The quiet, accurate nature of the bow and the ability to reload quickly allowed hunters the chance to make several kills at one time. The bows used by the Aboriginal people in Alberta were so powerful they have been seen to propel an arrow right through one buffalo and into a second one! The bow and arrow is relatively recent, first appearing in Alberta only about 1800 years ago.

The dart and throwing stick consists of a long, slender dart and a short, hand-held throwing stick. Known by the Aztec word *atlatl*, the throwing stick permitted darts to be thrown a great distance with considerable force, providing the hunters greater safety. This weapon followed the spear and was used from about 8000 to 2000 years ago.

Stone: A Tool for Every Use, A Use for Every Tool

Right:
Dozens of pieces of highly prized obsidian (volcanic glass) and chert were found buried in a pit on a farm near Milk River. These stones had been brought from Wyoming and Montana and cached for later use but apparently were forgotten. Age unknown.

Left:
Grooved cobbles of stone, called mauls, were tied to wooden handles and used like hammers (as illustrated below) to pound a variety of materials. The maul pictured here is from the Red Deer area; its age is unknown.

Right:
Shell fragments were cut, drilled and polished into jewelry and ornaments for clothing. These examples come from Junction site near Fort Macleod and the Ross site near Coaldale and are 500 years old.

Left:
The tiny size of this needle (2.7 cm), probably used to sew clothing, testifies not only to the skill of the person who made it but also to the skill of those who used it. This needle was found at the Stampede site in the Cypress Hills and is dated at 7300 years old.

Lower Right:
Beads used for ornamentation were made from hollow leg bones of birds and small mammals. A groove was etched around the circumference, and the bone was snapped in two. Trimming and polishing produced a smooth finish. The bone beads come from Head-Smashed-In Buffalo Jump and Junction Site near Fort Macleod. They are between 1000-500 years old.

Lower Left:
Sometimes artifacts were made of materials that conveyed a special symbolic meaning or value. This bone knife handle made of a bear jaw may have been meant to convey the awesome power of bear to the user. This handle is about 500 years old and comes from the Morkin site near Clareholm.

Fragile Things from the Past

Bone, shell and antler have properties very different from those of stone and were used to make tools for which stone was unsuitable. These materials can be cut, drilled, smoothed and shaped into delicate items that were not only functional but allowed the craftsman to express some artistic characteristics of the culture.

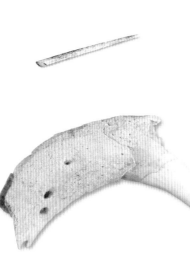

Ideas Preserved in Clay

Pottery was an invention that made it easier for Aboriginal people to cook and store food. Pots were made by shaping lumps of wet clay or by building up coils to the desired form. Final shaping was done by beating the outside of the vessel with a paddle, and decoration was added using fingers and tools to sculpt the surface. When dry, pots were hardened by baking in an open fire.

Fired to a hard state, pottery preserves well. Even if broken, it can be found and re-assembled into its original shape. Because pottery is fragile and heavy it was quickly abandoned when Europeans introduced the first copper kettles.

Alberta's pottery is part of a long tradition, used first over 4000 years ago in the southeastern United States. For much of its history, Alberta pottery is related to that of Saskatchewan and Manitoba. The earliest pottery in Alberta was produced around 1800 years ago and has been found in sites containing Avonlea arrow points. This pottery consists of simple, coconut-shaped vessels whose surfaces were impressed by a fabric-wrapped paddle. They were decorated with a single row of indentations, called punctuates, made by jabbing a stick or bone into the clay. Only fragments of these vessels have been found.

Following Avonlea culture, Old Women's culture began about 1200 years ago and lasted until European contact. Many archaeologists believe this culture represented the pre-contact Blackfoot peoples. Old Women's phase pottery shows increased complexity of vessel shape and decoration.

About 400 years ago, a new style of pottery appeared in Alberta. Known as Cluny pottery, the vessel shapes and decoration are quite complex. Vessel surfaces are impressed with paddles carved into squares, leaving a surface known as check-stamped. Brushing the surface with a stiff brush or impressing it with a toothed object—a dentate stamp—were favoured techniques. This general style of pottery can be traced through Saskatchewan to the farming villages in North and South Dakota. It is thought that Siouan-speaking people made the pottery. Its appearance may mark the migration of Assiniboine peoples, or perhaps Crow or Hidatsa, into the province.

Fingerprints Preserved in Clay: When decorating the outside of this pot, the potter braced the vessel on the inside, leaving fingerprints in the clay. Although such fingerprints are rare, they do have the potential to someday let archaeologists track the work of a single craftsperson. This pottery fragment with fingerprints was found at Bushfield West site, near Nipawin, Saskatchewan, and is dated at 350 years old.

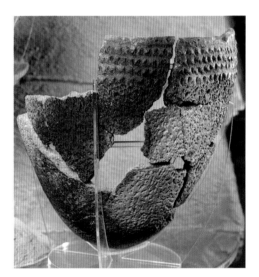

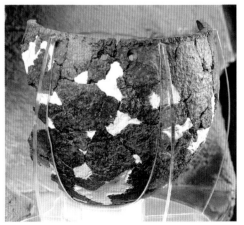

Top Left:
An unusual Avonlea culture pot was discovered near Head-Smashed-In Buffalo Jump. Dating to about 1200 years ago, this pot has a fabric-impressed surface but is conical in form instead of coconut-shaped and has three rows of fingernail impressions on the rim.

Bottom Left:
This pot has been reconstructed from pieces found at the Jenkin's Buffalo Jump near Stavely. Two paired holes are seen near the rim of the vessel, these were probably used to suspend the pot from a cord. It is of the Old Women's culture, a style of pottery made between 1200 and 250 years ago.

Hunting the Buffalo

Fletcher: An Ingenious Bison Kill

Right:
Provincial Museum of Alberta crew excavates 9000-year-old bison bones from thick mud at Fletcher site.

Below Right:
Spear points from the Fletcher Site. Age 9000 years old.

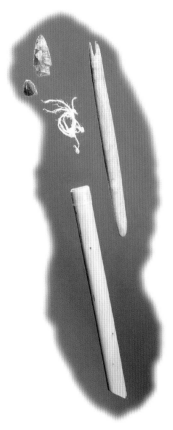

Spear-foreshaft Technology
Spears were deadly tools designed to allow rapid reloading. Stone tips were tied to a foreshaft that in turn was socketed into the end of a spear. After being plunged into the animal, the spear could be withdrawn and reloaded with a new tip. Hunters needed to carry only one spear and a quiver of foreshafts and points, reducing the weight of their weapons. Sinew and pine pitch would have been used for binding the points to the foreshaft.

For at least 10,000 years, the buffalo provided sustenance for people dwelling on the plains of Alberta. In order to commemorate this extraordinary relationship, the Syncrude Gallery of Aboriginal Culture has reconstructed the oldest bison kill site known in Alberta: the Fletcher Site. Located about 15 kilometres south of Taber near Chin Coulee, the Fletcher site is in a dry, unremarkable region of prairie. But 9000 years ago a lake existed here, and bison came to drink. A small ridge of land skirted the north edge of the lake and served to conceal the hunters who moved over the ridge and speared the huge beasts at water's edge. The success of this clever trap is indicated by a thick layer of bones buried in the mud of a farmer's dugout. These remains bear witness to the ingenuity of Alberta's earliest inhabitants. Here was not a chance encounter but a planned event directed by hunters to obtain a large supply of meat, fat and hides.

Fletcher Site diorama.

Nine thousand years ago, a band of hunters ambushed a herd of bison as they watered at a small lake. The hunters charge over a ridge, some throwing spears and others running in quickly to stab the animals. One bison, wounded in the lungs, attempts to escape along the shore. Crashing through the cattails, it is exhausted by the clinging mud. A young hunter pursues the bison. He hurriedly attempts to reload his spear by inserting the foreshaft with its stone spear point into a socket on the main shaft. He spills the contents of his quiver (other stone spear points, foreshafts, sinew, pine pitch and a knife). Responding to the danger from the bison's giant horns, an old hunter steps forward to deliver the killing blow. Further along the lake, other hunters have killed a female bison and are pursuing the calf. The rest of the herd has stampeded southward and is about to disappear into a coulee.

Buffalo Jumps

In seemingly serene hills, west of the town of Fort Macleod, countless buffalo were rounded up and driven over a precipice to their deaths. The site is known as Head-Smashed-In Buffalo Jump, and for nearly 6000 years this impressive site was used countless times to kill thousands of animals.

Aboriginal people organized buffalo jumps to kill large numbers of animals at one time. Often the hunt was done in the fall season to provide a surplus of food for the winter months. Locating and driving the animals would have taken between one and three days, depending on how far away the herd was from the cliff. The number of animals killed in one jump was probably between 100 and 200, because the most effective way of driving the animals over the cliff was in large numbers.

Bison hunters at Head-Smashed-In modified the land to fit their needs. An elaborate system of small piles of stone and brush called cairns were laid out in the shape of a huge funnel and were used to herd the bison towards the cliff. Investing the time and energy required to build such a substantial structure as a cairn network is a major commitment to a single place. Clearly, people intended to return to the site many times.

Once the herds of buffalo were located, it was the job of people called buffalo runners to herd the animals to the cliff using the drive lanes of cairns, a dangerous task requiring speed and skill. A favourite trick was to lure the buffalo using a calf disguise. Covered with a calf hide, a runner would imitate the bleating of a lost calf. The cows responded to this sound and caused the herd to turn and follow the runner in the direction of the cliff. Alexander Henry (the Elder), who witnessed an Assiniboine buffalo drive in 1776, testified to the skill with which the runners performed this mimicry: "Their gestures so closely resembled those of the animals themselves that had I not been in on the secret I should have been as much deceived as the buffalo."

Weary buffalo runners were joined by fresh waves of hunters who helped contain the animals within the cairn network and continued the relentless pressure. By the time they reached the edge of the cliff, the animals were stampeding too fast to stop.

Many buffalo were killed by the fall from the cliff, but those that were only stunned or wounded were killed on the ground. Hunters tried to kill all the buffalo, for they believed that escaped animals would mingle with new herds and warn them of the terrible trap. The Blackfoot word for a buffalo jump is *pis-kun* which translates as kettle of blood. The name, no doubt, was appropriate.

When the killing was over, the hunters faced the enormous task of converting the mound of carcasses into food and other supplies. Meat was cut into thin strips and then dried on wood frames. Drying not only preserved the meat but also greatly reduced its weight, making it easier to carry. Fats were mixed with dried, pounded meat to form pemmican. Slowly, after days or perhaps a week of butchering, people moved away from the buffalo jump.

Avonlea arrow points from Head-Smashed-In Buffalo Jump. Age 1800-500 years old.

Opposite:
The cliff at Head-Smashed-In Buffalo Jump.

Inset Opposite:
Drive lane cairns at Head-Smashed-In Buffalo Jump.

Above:
Buffalo pound model.

Inset Above:
A successful kill could result in the death of dozens, even hundreds, of animals at a single time, leaving a mass of bone for archaeologists to discover. This bone bed from the Smythe Pound site, near Pincher Creek, is 2600 years old. Courtesy of Environmental Management Associates.

The Buffalo Pound

The Buffalo Pound was another cunning trap where bison were driven into a wooden corral and killed. Pounds have been in use for at least 2000 years in western Canada and operated in much the same way as a buffalo jump.

Pounds were usually built on the downwind side of a small hill, hiding the pound from the bison and preventing the smell of the hunters from reaching the herd. Once such a place was found, it was used repeatedly for hundreds, even thousands of years. Many layers of bones in the soil are proof of the success of favoured sites. For both pounds and jumps the final stages of the drive were the most critical and the most dangerous. In both instances the stampeding bison were squeezed into a tighter and tighter space between the

converging lanes of rocks and brush. A wooden ramp was placed at the entrance to a pound making in almost impossible for the animals to jump back out.

Ancient pounds were flimsy constructions and could have easily been pushed over by stampeding bison. Hunters draped the side of the wooden corral with dark, hairy buffalo hides. This gave the pound the appearance of being solid, and the panicking bison ran in circles until they were killed.

Once the killing was over the meat and fat was made into pemmican to provide a high energy food supply for the long winter months.

Bones with Imbedded Stone Points

About 1300 years ago at the Women's Buffalo Jump site, near Cayley, a buffalo was struck in the front leg with a stone tipped arrow. The tip remained in the bone. The animal must have died immediately as there is no evidence that the wound around the arrow point began to heal.

New Ways of Processing Food

Broken stones and smashed bones may not look like artifacts, but they provide powerful evidence of an innovation in food processing that occurred nearly 5000 years ago—an ability to preserve food and store it for later consumption. While food had been cooked for thousands of years, the key to food preservation lay with the discovery of stone boiling.

Cooking pits were made in the ground using fresh animal hides and water. The pits of water were heated by adding red-hot rocks. Repeating this process eventually boiled the water. Bones were smashed to obtain marrow and then boiled in the cooking pits to remove additional fats. Meat was dried in the sun and smoked over fires, which preserved the meat and made it lighter and easier to carry. Fat was added to dried meat to make pemmican—a highly nutritious food that could be stored for many months. With preserved food available as a surplus, people were freed from the need to search daily for fresh food. More time could be spent on other aspects of life, such as playing games, telling stories, social activities and religious and spiritual pursuits, as well as specialized craft activities like stone and bone working and making clothing and pottery.

Top Right:
Bison bone with imbedded stone point circled in red.

Centre Right:
This pit, from Head-Smashed-In Buffalo Jump, was used to roast meat. It was lined with stones which may have been heated with a fire before the meat was put in. The meat was wrapped in vegetation to keep it clean and then buried in the pit. A fire was built on top of the pit to slowly roast the meat. This pit is 1200 years old.

Bottom Right:
Remains of a pit used to boil water and cook food. Head-Smashed-In Buffalo Jump, Fort Macleod. Age about 1000 years.

A Year in the Life

The Seasonal Round in Southern Alberta

Spring

As grass began to sprout on windswept, south-facing slopes, men were sent out to hunt the buffalo attracted to the new green grass, and people moved up on to the plains to avoid the cold, damp and possible flooding in the river valleys. Gear and clothing were repaired in anticipation of summer travel. People might also visit a medicine wheel memorial and pray for good fortune.

Summer

In summer, people camped along the edges of river valleys where the wind kept mosquitoes and biting flies away. They broke up into small camps, often composed of extended families. Since the buffalo had to return to the rivers to water, small parties of hunters could ambush them in the rough breaks and gullies along the valley edges. As well, valley plants such as berries could be harvested from these locations. People were highly mobile at this time of year, moving camp every few days but always staying close to water.

People did not wander aimlessly over the plains during ancient times. Rather, they moved in a logical manner to harvest a variety of resources as they became available with the changing of the seasons. Archaeologists call this movement the seasonal round.

Fall

Many bands would gather together in the fall to operate a communal bison kill. A buffalo jump required many hunters and great organization. The herds had to be driven towards the jump by young men who encircled the herd and caused them to stampede in the desired direction. Meat was dried and made into pemmican to be used during winter when game was scarce and hunting difficult. In fall, fine quality stone for tools was mined in the mountains before snow covered the ground.

Winter

Wood was a requisite for winter camping, so the bands camped in wooded river valleys in the plains, foothills and parklands. Since dead branches and trees were used for firewood, campsites had to be located in different locales every winter to ensure adequate supplies of deadwood. Fresh meat was hunted whenever possible, but dry meat and pemmican stores were available should the weather be bad or the buffalo distant. The long winter evenings were enlivened with feasting, story-telling, gambling games, and more serious recounting of stories, legends and tales to inspire and teach the young.

A Remarkable Dwelling

Overlooking the Oldman River near Taber, the 5000-year-old Cranford site contains some of the earliest evidence for the use of the tipi in Alberta. Earlier Aboriginal groups must have had shelters, but there is little evidence of what these may have looked like. Presence of the tipi is indicated by conspicuous rings of rocks, which were used to hold down the bottom of the hide dwelling. The Cranford site must have been a favoured location for camping by Plains people, as the archaeological evidence indicates that people returned to this place to camp right up until the last few hundred years.

The tipi was a remarkable invention. With movable flaps at the top, and liners along the inside poles, smoke from fires was channeled out the top of the tipi. Tipis could be put up or taken down in minutes and accommodated eight to 10 people. There are tens of thousands of tipi rings in Alberta. Most tipis were occupied only a day or two before people moved on to new camping places. Thus, even a small group of people could make dozens of new tipi rings each year. The rings were also re-used when people returned to a previous camping place. Most tipi rings contain few artifacts and cannot be dated.

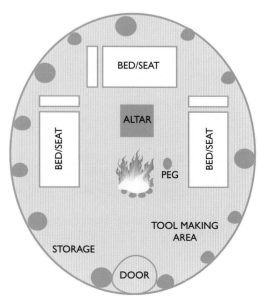

The Sacred World

Medicine Wheels: A Sacred Landscape

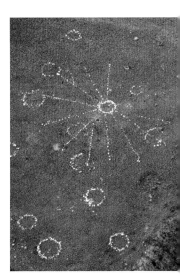

Left:
The Many-Spotted-Horses Medicine Wheel, on the Blood (Kainai) Reserve, was made within the past 150 years in honour of a great chief.

Below:
Aerial view of the Ellis Medicine Wheel, north of Medicine Hat. Age about 500 years. Courtesy John Brumley.

Medicine wheels acquired that name because they were said to be powerful places (medicine) and because some of them have spoke-like lines of rocks (wheel). There are about 70 wheels known in North America, most of them, 50, are in southern and central Alberta. Medicine wheels occur in many different shapes, and some are thousands of years old.

A medicine wheel is defined as any structure that consists of at least two of the following three traits: (1) a central stone cairn, (2) one or more concentric stone circles, and/or (3) two or more stone lines radiating outward from a central point. Based on artifacts excavated from medicine wheel sites, archaeologists have determined they were in use from 4500 years ago until European contact. This long period of use suggests that the specific rituals and ceremonies conducted at these sites may have varied over time.

Some medicine wheels were made by the Kainai (Blood) people this century. According to Native elders, these recent wheels were built to commemorate the lives of great hunters or brave warriors. Some astronomers have argued that medicine wheels were ancient observatories, built to chart seasonal events of stars. Despite the debate over their function, one thing is certain: medicine wheels were probably always sacred places, built and used for matters pertaining to the spiritual world. They formed part of a sacred landscape.

Vision quest site near Head-Smashed-In Buffalo Jump. Age unknown.

Cairns

Cairns (rock piles), such as this one from Canadian Forces Base Suffield, are a common archaeological site in Alberta. They range from a few rocks to huge constructions containing thousands of head-sized stones. Long lines of cairns served as drive lanes to direct buffalo to kill sites. Some served as traps for small game, markers for trails, memorials to hunting success, or for storage of food and tools. Contrary to popular belief, cairns almost never mark the location of human burials.

Above:
Suffield Cairn. Age unknown.

Below:
Effigy near Rumsey. Age unknown.

Effigies

Lines of rocks are sometimes laid out on the ground to resemble human beings. Although rare in Alberta, these effigies are occasionally found on the Plains and in the parkland. Some effigies are said to commemorate the death of an individual; others represent Napi, the Blackfoot trickster and hero.

Vision Quest

Perched on high hills and in remote locations are small structures of stone called vision quest sites. These ancient sites, found in southern and central Alberta, mark the place where Aboriginal people communicated with the spirit world. Most are oval in shape and are made of rocks stacked to make a shallow enclosure large enough for a single person to lie down. Here one would stay, abstaining from food and water, for a period of four days. Spirits communicated with them through a series of visions. In these visions people received power or knowledge from the spirits, were told the future, were healed of sickness, or made peace with themselves. Most vision quest sites cannot be dated, but it is clear that vision questing is an ancient activity. It is also a modern one. Aboriginal people still use ancient vision quest sites and create new ones.

Objects of Art

Aboriginal art took many forms, including objects carved out of soft stone, bone or antler, as well as paintings and carvings on rock walls. Carved objects are rare, but a few examples have been found. Carvings generally take the form of animals, although some figures are of humans or other unrecognizable creatures.

Most pieces of art also had spiritual power, including the carved imagery found on functional tools. For example, a slender piece of stone was tied to a hunting weapon to allow a hunter to throw a dart farther and with greater accuracy. The purpose of the stone was to add extra weight to the weapon, yet sometimes these slender stones were decorated with the images of animals, which provided spiritual power to the weapon.

Art Painted and Carved onto Rocks

Scenes that have been painted or etched onto rock surfaces are relatively common in Alberta. Generally called rock art, these provocative images provide a glimpse into the artistic culture of ancient peoples. Some figures are carved or etched into the rock surface, presumably using a pointed piece of bone, antler or stone (petroglyphs). Usually only the outline of a human or animal was carved out, but in a few cases the entire body of the figure was scooped or pecked out of the rock. These pecked-out figures are rare and are believed to be the oldest rock art in Alberta.

Another method of making art was to paint images onto the rock surface (pictographs). Red ochre, a mineral rich in iron, was mixed with fat, and the resulting paint was applied to the rock walls with fingers or the soft, porous ends of bones. This ancient and sacred paint has lasted for thousands of years.

The remote and spectacular locations at which rock art is found suggest that the place the art was made could have been almost as important as the images themselves. Aboriginal people may have gone to these remote places in order to communicate with the spirit world, and one way to do so was to make images on the rocks.

Sometimes rock art is narrative, it tells a story—capturing a horse, a battle between two groups, hunting an animal. Other rock art is ceremonial—an attempt to communicate with the spirit world, and often it came from dreams or visions. Like all art, these ancient images are open to many interpretations. Contemporary Aboriginal people still have a strong spiritual attachment to ancient rock art sites, and much has been learned about the meaning of rock art from Native elders. However, the meaning of some rock art will remain forever in the visions and dreams of its creators.

Left:
Carved Bison from Ardmore near St. Paul, age unknown.

Below Left:
Chipped stone image of bison. Location and age unknown.

Above:
This evocative painting shows a human body with an animal-like head, holding what are probably rattles. West of Stavely.

Above Top:
A red ochre painting near Canmore shows a human holding a circular object, probably a ceremonial hoop or drum.

Below Left:
Row of human figures pecked into the soft sandstone at Writing-On-Stone Provincial Park, near Milk River. Courtesy of Michael Klassen.

Fishing Camp Diorama.

BIRCH
MOUNTAIN
SITE

The scene depicted in the Fish Camp Diorama is set in the Birch Mountains of northeastern Alberta on the edge of a small stream that drains Eaglenest Lake.

Ancient Ways of Living
Fish Camp – A Northern Way of Life

The spring fish runs were a welcome part of northern life. They provided much-needed food and a chance for many social activities. About 1000 years ago a group of families gathered on the banks of a stream that drains Eaglenest Lake in the Birch Mountains of northern Alberta. These hunters and gatherers, who spent much of the long, cold winter spread out in small groups across the northern bush, are able to come together and visit because of a plentiful, predictable supply of food. From late April to late May, different kinds of fish, such as pike, walleye and suckers, rush up rivers and streams by the thousands to lay their eggs. During this time, people can eat their fill of fresh fish and roe and preserve large quantities of food by smoking and drying fillets on racks. They also can take the time to visit family and friends, trade for various items, and make plans for the coming summer months. Gatherings like the one pictured here could have happened any spring from a few hundred to a few thousand years ago, and scores or even hundreds of people could have been involved.

Using a leister—a spear made with a shaft of wood and prongs of antler or bone—a woman snags a big pike and flips it out of the water. Behind the woman most of the fish are caught by being swept into the weir, or fish trap. The weir is constructed of a loose dam of rocks and logs and a fence of sloping, pointed stakes. The slope of the stakes allows the fish to swim in with the rush of the stream but then keeps them penned. The holes in the dam let the water pass through so it does not overflow. Once in the weir, the fish are grabbed or flipped onto shore by hand.

On shore, to the left of the weir, women are preparing the fish by slicing them open with hafted stone knives and removing their entrails. The split and cleaned fish are either cooked and eaten right away or preserved for future meals. Behind the cleaning scene, fillets are being roasted over a fire. Farther away, an elderly woman watches carefully as split fish are smoked on a rack. On an adjacent rack, more fish dry in the springtime sun.

Both dried fish and smoked fish can be kept for months and will be an important source of food once the spawning run has ended. Dry fish can be pounded into a powder in rawhide basins and mixed with fat to produce a compact, high-energy food.

A few other activities are going on in this camp. In front of the lodges off to the left, a birchbark canoe is being sealed with pine or spruce pitch mixed with bitumen from the tar sands, a very effective glue. The same glue was used to haft the stone knives into their wooden handles in the foreground scene. To the right of the stream, an adult and youth return to camp with some hares they have snared using hide thongs, sinew or strands of hair.

The Genius of Simplicity

Aboriginal people began inhabiting the northern forests immediately after the Ice Age glaciers retreated from the area some 11,000 years ago. The boreal forest environment is a difficult one for human survival because of severe weather, limited plant foods, numerous insects and the solitary habits of large game animals. Despite these conditions, Aboriginal people developed a profoundly successful adaptation to the northern forests. Far from being isolated, people living in the boreal forest were in contact with cultures stretching from the Plains to further north.

Most archaeological sites in the boreal forest are found near lakes and rivers. Here, groups of small sites tell of a lifestyle based on hunting large game, fishing, and snaring small animals. Unfortunately, preservation of artifacts is poor in the forest, leaving little archaeological evidence of these ancient people. Also, the isolation and difficult access to northern regions has limited the amount of archaeological work. Much less is known about northern peoples than those from the Plains and parkland regions.

Northern Life Through the Seasons

From the extremes of darkness, deep snow and bitter cold in winter to long, hot days in summer, life in northern Alberta presented many challenges to ancient Aboriginal people. They had to acquire adequate food, shelter and tools, and needs and supplies changed with the seasons.

There was plenty to eat in the northern bush, but resources are spread thinly over large distances. Some foods are available only in certain seasons or at certain places. To make matters more complicated, some animals (like hare and moose) might be numerous one year, but hard to find the next. To survive, hunters and gatherers had to read the environment as it changed through the year to know where to go to get the food and raw materials they needed. Their travels were patterned according to what the seasons had to offer. This seasonal round would vary from year to year, depending on the abundance and timing of resources and the interests of the people.

Travel capability also played a part in defining seasonal movements. During the seasons of open waters, it was possible to move far and fast by canoe. In the winter, people were restricted to foot-power, usually on snowshoes, so the distances that could be travelled were limited.

The low population density across the northern bush also influenced travel patterns. For most of the year, groups travelled light and usually consisted of only one or a few related families. Periodically these groups wanted to meet so they could visit friends and family, swap stories, learn about goings-on elsewhere, trade for goods and look for potential spouses.

Spring fish runs provided an opportunity for larger numbers of people to gather together for a couple of weeks. Dependable concentrations of food were few and far

between in the northern bush, so people took advantage of such short-term surpluses to congregate in one spot.

Migrating herds of woodland caribou provided another opportunity for bands to gather together. In early winter and late spring, hunters would trick and drive these herds into large wooden corrals where they could be speared or snared by their antlers. Huge flocks of migrating birds stopping over at lakes during spring and fall would also have attracted larger groups of people. Summer may have seen people gathering at good fishing lakes for a few weeks or picking berries together.

In the long winter, when food became scarcer, lone hunters followed the solitary moose or small herds of wapiti, deer or wood bison, while women snared fur-bearers to make clothing. Being spread out in smaller groups over the landscape ensured that enough food was available to make it through to spring.

Below:
Barbed bone point from Little Whitefish Lake used to spear fish and probably muskrat and beaver. Its age is unknown.

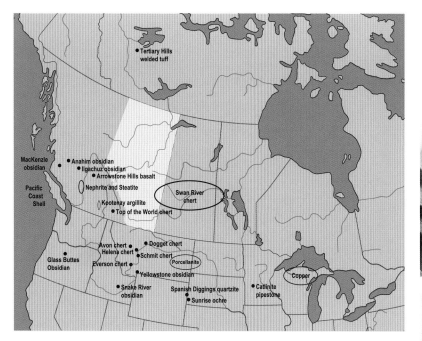

Networks of Ancient Trade

Long before Europeans came to Alberta, Aboriginal people were engaged in active trade with neighbouring groups and obtained goods and services not available where they lived. Virtually all aspects of culture were exchanged, from simple goods like stone and shell to marriage partners, songs, medicines and religious ceremonies. Trade created important social relationships and probably led to both war and peace. An artifact was likely an article of trade if it was found far from its place of origin. Scientific analysis of trace elements in stone and metals can be used to pinpoint the specific sources of some of these materials. With obsidian, for example, analyses can detect not only the region of origin but the exact volcano from which the volcanic glass originated. There is evidence of trade between Aboriginal groups dating back thousands of years and extending for thousands of kilometres. Trade went in all directions: north to the Subarctic, west to the Pacific Ocean, east to the Great Lakes and the Missouri River, and south to the Great Basin and southern Plains.

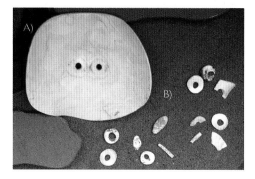

Unfortunately, much of what was traded left no trace at pre-contact archaeological sites. Typically, only durable items like stone and shell are preserved. Yet these few items provide the key to an elaborate network of exchange and allow archaeologists to determine what was traded, where, and with whom. In Alberta, trade goods of various materials are often found that were not available here, such as stone used for making pipes, obsidian, copper and seashell. But what did the Aboriginal people of Alberta offer in return? One likely commodity would have been the vast surplus of meat, hide and pemmican obtained from such sites as Head-Smashed-In Buffalo Jump.

The People of the Past

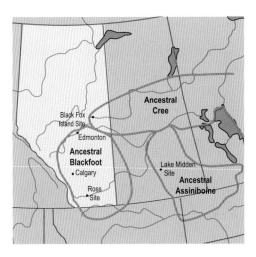

These Blackfoot arrow points have curved bases and shallow notches and were found at the Ross site, near Coaldale. The pottery found with them has thick walls and decoration made with finger pinches. These artifacts are 500 years old.

These Assiniboine arrow points have straight, square bases and deep, narrow notches and are from Lake Midden site, Saskatchewan. The pottery found with them has thin walls and elaborate decoration. These artifacts are 400 years old.

These Cree arrow points have narrow bases and broad, shallow notches and were found at Black Fox Island site, Lac La Biche. The pottery from the same site has thin walls and simple decoration including perforations around the neck. These artifacts are 450 years old.

Aboriginal history extends back at least 11,000 years and most of it is shrouded in mystery. For much of this vast time period we will never know the tribal names of the people of the past. One of the most fascinating questions about the past is also the most difficult to answer: Who were the people who left behind these archaeological sites and artifacts? Can we assign names like Blackfoot, Cree or Beaver to artifacts that are hundreds, even thousands, of years old? Many artifacts made by Aboriginal people, such as hide scrapers, hardly changed over 11,000 years. These tools are of no help in distinguishing specific tribal groups. But some artifacts did change through time and over geographic space. Stone arrow points and pottery from different areas of Alberta look somewhat different, indicating that they might have been made by a variety of tribal groups.

Based on artifact style, archaeologists have identified three groups of people that lived in central and southern Alberta during the last 650 years. These groups are believed to be the ancestors of the Blackfoot, Cree and Assiniboine people. Arrow points show slight differences in their bases and notches. Pottery from each of the three regions also shows varying manufacturing and decorating techniques. These may express the individual styles of distinct groups of people.

Right:
The Cluny site on the Bow River.
Note circular depressions.

Right:
The Cluny site on the Bow River.
Note circular depressions.

Above:
An unusual pottery style reveals
that the occupants of the Cluny
site came from North Dakota. This
example of Cluny pottery comes
from the Cluny site on the Siksika
Reserve and is 250 years old.

One Gun: Strangers from the South

At the dawn of written history a new group
of people arrived on the northern Plains,
bringing with them unique possessions and
a different lifestyle. However, within a few
years they had vanished.

Although population movements have
occurred throughout Aboriginal history, a
clearly understood one occurred in the
archaeological period called One Gun. For
once archaeologists know when a move
happened, from where the people came, and
who the people were. But we don't know
what happened to them.

About 400 years ago, Siouan-speaking
people from the Missouri River region of
North Dakota began moving north and
west, arriving in Alberta about 250 years
ago. They lived in large earthen huts and
grew domesticated crops of corn, beans and
squash. No such people had ever lived in
Alberta before.

These Siouan people brought with them a
distinctive style of pottery, unusual
dwellings, unique food-storage pits, and
artifacts that link them to a Missouri River
homeland. However, attempts at agriculture

must have failed, and these people either
died out, moved away or blended in with
other Aboriginal groups. By the time the
first Europeans arrived, about 1754, these
strangers had disappeared.

The Cluny Site

The best evidence for the presence of a
Siouan-speaking group in Alberta comes
from the Cluny site located on the Siksika
Reserve east of Calgary. The architecture of
the site and the artifacts recovered from the
excavations indicate a homeland in the
Missouri River region of North Dakota. For
protection from enemies, the Cluny site had
a trench dug around it and a palisade wall
of timbers. The circular pits may have been
small earthen houses or pits in which to
hide from enemy arrows and bullets.

The Shadow of the Europeans

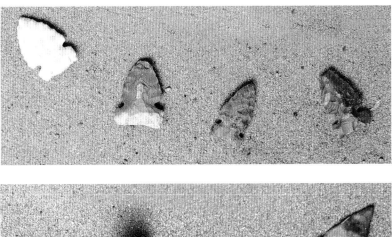

Alberta was a long distance from the first European settlements to the east (French and English) and to the south (Spanish); therefore it was among the last places to be explored by Europeans. However, long-established Aboriginal trade networks brought European goods to the heart of the continent, signalling important changes in Native culture. Some European items were considered better than previously used tools. Metal pots, for example, replaced earthen pottery so quickly that memories of pottery making rapidly faded from Aboriginal culture. Only through archaeological study has ancient pottery making been recovered.

In other cases, traditional methods were preferred over European ways. Native people continued to use the bow and arrow for most hunting. Armed with a bow and arrow, a hunter on horseback could rapidly reload and kill many more animals than was possible with a slow and awkward muzzle-loading rifle.

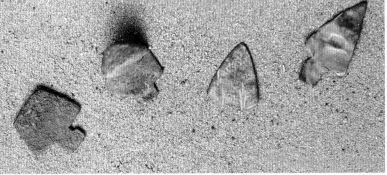

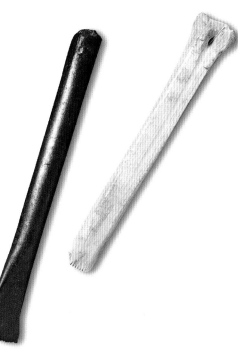

Above:
Stone arrow points broke easily and were difficult to repair. Metal points would bend and could be hammered back into shape. For these reasons, metal was preferred for making arrowheads. These artifacts are from the Morkin site, near Claresholm, and date to about 250 years ago.

Lower left:
European items were changed to suit the desires of Aboriginal people. Scraps of metal were formed into cone-shaped ornaments, replacing hard-to-get shells traded from the Pacific coast. The age of these dentalia shells from the northwest coast is unknown. Metal tinklers from Fort George, near Elk Point, are 200 years old.

Lower Right:
For thousands of years, leg bones of large mammals were shaped into tools used for cleaning hides. This bone flesher comes from Fort White Earth, near Smoky Lake, and is about 200 years old. After European contact, barrels from old guns were made into hide fleshers. This example is about 150 years old.

The Past Becomes the Present

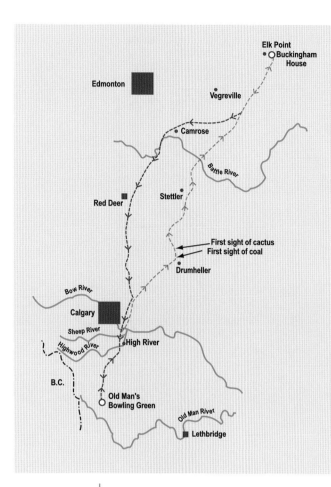

Near the Battle River, Fidler identifies a group of people called the Sessew. These people must be the Sarcee (now called Tsuu T'ina).

"At noon met a good number of Sessew Indians going to the House to trade...gave them each a little bit of Tobacco, which they were much in want of."

Camped near the Sheep River, Fidler tells of the fate of a Flat-head boy.

"There is a Flat-head boy of a different Tribe at the Tents, whom they caught stealing horses...Several of our Indians wish him to be killed, but our Chief says no & that he shall be sent safely away to his own country."

At the Highwood River, Fidler joins a large band of Muddy River Indians. This group is now known to be the Piikani (Peigan).

"[I] arrived at the Spitcheyee [Highwood] river at Noon & found nearly 150 Tents of Muddy river Indians that had been here for many Days."

On the Oldman River, Fidler becomes the first European to meet the Kootenay.

"Men say that a few tents of the Cottonahew Indians are at the [Oldman] river wishing our Indians to visit them with Goods ...[They] have] never seen a European before."

Camped near the Bow River, Fidler meets a Snake Indian. The identity of the Snake remains a mystery: some think the Snake are Shoshoni; others think they are Siouan people.

"At last we found out that a Snake Indian man was near... & in 1/4 of an hour... all the men formed into a large ring & the Snake Indian in the middle, all smoking together in friendship."

Above:
In 1792-93 fur trader and explorer Peter Fidler travelled with the Piikani (Peigan) from Edmonton to southwestern Alberta and back. His journal provides important information on the names and locations of Aboriginal groups in Alberta. Some of these are recognizable as Native groups we know today. Others remain a mystery.

The first written accounts of Aboriginal people—their names, territories, customs and artifacts—are of enormous use to archaeologists. These documents provide clues as to where archaeological sites will be found, how specific artifacts were made and used, and the meaning of unusual sites such as medicine wheels and vision quests. Historical records are especially useful in identifying the territory occupied by different tribal groups. This information helps determine which tribal group created specific archaeological sites.

The first Europeans venturing into the homelands of Aboriginal people were in unfamiliar territory, and they may have misidentified certain places. Also, Europeans usually travelled with one specific Native group, and this group influenced the names of places and people recorded by the Europeans.

Europeans also brought with them biases about Aboriginal people (such as Aboriginal culture being inferior to European culture).

The Horse

Horses transformed life on the northern Plains. Changing how people hunted, travelled and transported their belongings, they allowed people to come together in larger numbers for ceremonies and created new distinctions in wealth and status.

Horses gave hunters greater range, mobility and independence. Where the buffalo pound and jump required careful planning and the efforts of an entire community, horses enabled small groups of mounted hunters to obtain meat and hides more quickly.

Horses also allowed people to transport, and hence own, more items. When moving camp, women tied parfleches and saddlebags filled with dried food and clothing onto packhorses. They packed children and bulky household furnishings onto horse-pulled travois. Thus loaded, a single horse could haul up to 500 pounds.

The material benefits that horses brought formed the basis for new distinctions in wealth and status. Horse-rich families enjoyed a higher standard of living and often held prominent positions in ceremonial and political life. People with fewer horses relied on dogs to carry their gear and on wealthy neighbors to share meat.

Deep respect for the horse inspired the production of elaborate horse trappings. Although saddles, stirrups, and bridles had their origins in Spanish riding gear, Aboriginal people created their own distinctive style of horse ornamentation. The style of saddle shown here was used by women when riding and when packing gear on horses. A blanket placed under the saddle protected the horse's back.

Left:
Horse bridle. Braided horse hair. Northern Plains. Late 1800s.

Below :
Woman's saddle, with stirrups and saddle blanket. Wood, rawhide, tanned hide and glass beads. Kainai. Circa 1910.

The Fur Trade

Above:
The Archithinue camp, based on Henday's journals. Henday diorama.

Two trade systems met in Alberta in the 1700s. One was the long-established exchange network of Native North America. The other was a market-oriented system financed and organized by Europeans. Together, they created the northwestern fur trade.

Europeans began to tap the vast fur resources of interior North America in the late 1600s. By the mid-1700s, British entrepreneurs had established trading posts along Hudson Bay and James Bay, while French traders had begun building competing posts on the Saskatchewan River. But it was Aboriginal trade routes and contacts that carried the fur trade into the interior. Travelling familiar routes, Cree and Nakoda traders brought metal goods and cloth to Alberta decades before the first European arrived. These same middlemen transported furs back to the European posts. They set the terms of trade and told European traders what types of goods they should offer.

Middlemen lost their influence once Europeans began building inland posts in the late 1700s. But Aboriginal people's knowledge of resources, people and places remained essential to the fur trade's success.

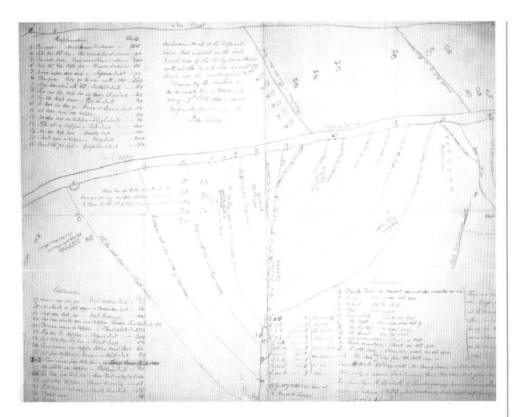

Top:
"An Indian Map of the Different Tribes that inhabit on the South & West side of the Rocky Mountains..."
Drawn by Ak ko mo ki and copied by Peter Fidler, 1801. Courtesy Hudson's Bay Company Archives, Provincial Archives of Manitoba.

Alliances and the Fur Trade

Aboriginal people viewed trade as part of broader social and political relationships. People might trade for articles they didn't particularly value in order to promote friendly relations with another band or nation. Often, they sealed alliances through marriage or adoption. They established far-reaching networks that eased the movement of people and goods.

European traders had to respect the protocol that surrounded trade and alliance building. They relied on Aboriginal peacemakers to negotiate the alliances that made the fur trade's expansion possible and entered into marriages of their own with Aboriginal women.

Trading relationships were established and renewed through ceremonies. Men known as trading captains headed the parties going to the trading posts. They spoke on behalf of their groups, prepared the grand pipe (calumet), and presented European traders with gifts of beaver pelts and buffalo robes.

In return, the Europeans gave gifts of tobacco, blankets and clothing.

In some instances, the fur trade strengthened existing alliances. The Cree and Nakoda (Assiniboine) likely became allies in the late 1500s or early 1600s. They cemented their alliance through the exchange of guns and horses, the former acquired by the Cree through trade at Hudson's Bay and the latter acquired by the Nakoda from sources further south. Pooling their resources, travelling together, and marrying one another, they maintained an advantageous middleman position vis-a-vis other groups involved in the western fur trade for well over a century.

and returned to tell of his exploits. A journal attributed to him (likely composed by others working from Henday's written or oral account) provides the earliest written record about the Aboriginal people of Alberta.

After four months of travel Henday arrived at a huge encampment—200 tipis, some 1600 individuals—located near present-day Red Deer. He had reached the territory of a people he called the Archithinue, the Cree word for stranger. Most historians believe that he sat down to negotiate with the powerful Blackfoot Nation.

Henday and Attickasish, the Cree trading captain who acted as his guide and interpreter, were called to the Archithinue leader's tipi. A feast was held, pipes smoked, speeches made and gifts exchanged. Only then did Henday ask the Archithinue leader to bring his furs to Hudson Bay. The response was swift and clear. The leader said that his people could not live without buffalo meat, would not leave their horses, and did not know how to paddle canoes. Henday noted that these comments were "exceedingly true." The following spring he returned to Hudson Bay with a flotilla of Cree trading canoes, his mission a failure.

Some of Henday's notes are difficult to interpret. In one entry, he describes the Archithinue camp: We "came to 200 tents of Archithinue natives, pitched in two rows, and an opening in the middle; where we were conducted to the Leader's tent." However, of the thousands of tipi ring sites recorded by archaeologists on the Alberta Plains, none conforms to this two-row pattern. Oral tradition among Plains peoples indicates that large camps were arranged in a circular fashion. Historical photographs generally show tipis arranged in clusters that do not conform to any strict pattern. Paintings and later nineteenth century photographs of Sioux camps, on the other hand, do show linear tipi arrangements. Perhaps the Archithinue were a more southern Plains people. Alternatively, the two rows to which Henday referred may have been the inner and outer rings of a large camp circle.

Anthony Henday and the Archithinue, 1754

For seventy years after its arrival at York Factory along the shores of Hudson Bay, the Hudson's Bay Company encouraged Aboriginal people to bring furs to its trading posts along the Bay. But as local animal populations declined, it became necessary to contact more distant groups. Independent French traders based in Montreal saw the potential for inland trade and by the mid-1700s were moving into the interior of western Canada. Faced with competition, the Company commissioned a young employee named Anthony Henday to venture into the uncharted territories of Saskatchewan and Alberta. His mission: find the buffalo-hunting peoples of the Prairies and convince them to bring furs to Hudson Bay.

It was a remarkable journey—a solitary European led across thousands of kilometres of unmapped territory by dozens of Cree and Nakoda middlemen. Travelling by canoe, on foot and on horseback, Henday finally met the Plains First Nations

Henday's meeting with the Archithinue was an important historical event. His lack of success in encouraging trade with Europeans reveals that the First Nations of the interior were self-sustaining and already had successful trade networks in place. They did not need European goods, although they acquired them when the opportunity arose. The meeting also symbolized the encounter of Aboriginal and European cultures, an encounter that would change the course of historical events in western Canada.

Aboriginal People and the Fur Trade

Aboriginal people's contributions to the fur trade extended far beyond procuring pelts. They constructed snowshoes, dog sleds and birch bark canoes, each key to travel in the north. Guides introduced traders to the best travel routes and helped them find their way across the continent. Local hunters provided fresh game, fowl and fish for employees at fur trade posts. They also supplied large quantities of dried meat and fish to feed the voyageurs who worked on the fur trade's boat brigades. Fur trade personnel could experience extreme privation if they failed to secure a hunter's services.

> "Mr. McDougald and his men were reduced to the necessity of eating their Parchment Sled Wrappers and would in all probability have perished had they not met the English Chief [a Chipewyan leader] who directed them to a cache of meat."
>
> Hudson's Bay Company Governor-in-Chief George Simpson, February 13, 1821.

Women were major contributors to the fur trade. They prepared pelts and hides for trade, dried meat and fish, collected berries and other country foods, and made the pemmican that was the fur trade brigades' staple food. They also trapped smaller fur-bearing animals, such as rabbit and marten, and brought them into the posts to trade on

their own account. Those who married fur trade company employees had a particularly close involvement with the trade. Wives netted the snowshoes that made winter travel possible and sewed hide moccasins for post employees. They cleaned and tanned some of the pelts brought in for trade and collected and processed country foods. They tended fishnets, split and dried the fish they caught, cared for gardens planted at the larger posts and kept the posts clean. Fur traders' wives and daughters also brought useful diplomatic skills to the posts where they lived, acting as interpreters and intermediaries between traders and Aboriginal groups.

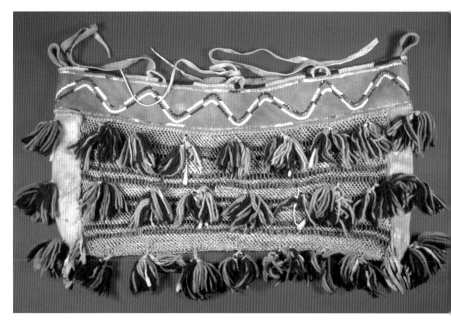

Above:
Game bag. Moose hide, babiche, porcupine quills and yarn. Late 1800s. Hunters packed small game and fowl in these bags. Métis.

Below:
Keskarrah and his daughter Green Stockings. Based on a watercolour by Robert Hood. 1823. Courtesy National Archives of Canada C-005528.

Keskarrah worked as a guide and provisioner for Sir John Franklin's expeditions in the Great Slave Lake area. His daughter is shown mending a snowshoe.

New Things for Old Needs

Aboriginal people used European goods selectively. They had perfected articles to meet their needs and did not require European trade goods to survive. In many cases, Aboriginal traders accepted European goods as luxury items to trade with other Aboriginal people. In this way, European trade items became incorporated into extensive Aboriginal trade networks.

Aboriginal people evaluated European articles in terms of the amount of labour (as measured in furs or provisions) it took to acquire them. For the most part, they continued to use their own articles, adding European goods to their belongings when it suited them.

People often modified European trade goods to serve familiar functions. They cut up copper kettles and barrel hoops into metal arrowheads. They flattened the end of gun barrels to make hide fleshers, made hooded overcoats known as capotes from trade blankets, and attached sewing thimbles and coins to clothing as adornment.

Below:
The Hudson's Bay Company post at Lac La Biche. 1895. Sketch by Frederick Remington. Courtesy Glenbow Archives.

Lac La Biche was one of Alberta's earliest communities. It was founded by two freeman families, the Desjarlais and the Cardinals, who settled in the area in the first decade of the 1800s.

The New People: The Métis

When fur trade companies began building posts inland, they brought west a labour force composed of men from French Canada and the British Isles. Many of these men married local Aboriginal women and raised families at the posts where they were stationed. Although most left when their term of service ended, some stayed on as "freemen", becoming independent hunters, trappers and traders. They and their families formed the nucleus of Alberta's first Métis communities.

Maintaining close links with First Nations bands and with trading company personnel, the freemen and their families moved easily in both spheres. The companies appreciated their versatility and recruited

fort hunters, trappers and trading captains from among their ranks. Entire families participated in the trade, with individual members pursuing activities that best suited their interests and skills.

The 1821 merger of the North West and Hudson's Bay Companies and the accompanying cessation of their fierce rivalry weakened the freemen's bargaining position. The HBC's monopolistic control of the trade meant that the services of these intermediaries were no longer essential, and many families found themselves cut off. Some moved east to Red River (present-day Winnipeg), where the HBC had set aside land for retired company employees and their families. But many chose to stay in Alberta. Here, united by ties of kinship and shared experience, they founded culturally distinctive communities in such diverse locales as Lac La Biche, Lesser Slave Lake, Lac Ste. Anne and Fort Vermilion.

Epidemic Disease

Epidemic diseases of European origin, such as smallpox, measles and influenza, had a devastating impact on Aboriginal populations. They reached Alberta before Europeans themselves did, moving along the same routes of trade and travel as the horse and gun. Initial epidemics were particularly deadly, as previously unexposed populations had no resistance to the new pathogens that they encountered. Some groups lost up to 90 percent of their people. With such large-scale loss of life, much cultural knowledge, too, was lost.

Traditional herbal and spiritual treatments had little impact against the new diseases. Neither did European purges, plasters and salves. With everyone ill, no one could care for the sick or bring water and firewood to camp. Some people survived the initial onslaught only to die because there were no healthy hunters left to provide food.

Smallpox vaccination checked the spread of at least one epidemic. In 1837, officers at several fur trade posts vaccinated visiting Aboriginal traders. Plains Cree at Fort Pelly, Saskatchewan, learned the procedure and took vaccine back to their communities. While some Plains groups lost up to 75 percent of their people in the smallpox epidemic that year, the Plains Cree escaped largely unscathed.

Tragically, however, the fur trade contributed more often to the spread of disease than to its eradication. The 1835 influenza epidemic, for example, was carried by the Athabasca boat brigade bringing winter supplies from Norway House to Fort Chipewyan. Post journals document the disease's spread from one community to another in the wake of the brigade's passage upriver.

Decline of Animal Populations

To most Europeans, the Northwest seemingly contained an endless amount of furs. But major fur and game animal populations declined quickly under the trade's relentless pressure. In 1792, the North West Company built Fort George along the North Saskatchewan River to harvest the wealth of the surrounding "rich and plentiful Country, abounding with all kinds of animals especially Beavers & Otters." Just three years later, company trader Duncan M'Gillivray wrote that the "Country around… is now entirely ruined." Such rapid depletion of animal resources created hardships for Aboriginal people and threw fur trade enterprises into turmoil.

The situation was most desperate in the North. Wood buffaloes, on which the Tsatu of the Peace River country depended, had been nearly exterminated by the 1830s as the result of pressure to provide meat for the northern fur trade brigades. Other food and fur animals had also become scarce. In 1823 Edward Smith, Chief Factor at Fort Chipewyan, reported that entire bands were close to starvation, "their Country exhausted of Beaver and large Animals, and by who? by the Wild, ambitious policy of the Whites Who study their own interest first and then that of the Natives."

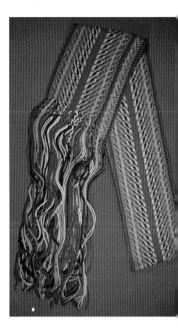

Below:
Sash. Métis. Post-1850.

Colourful "L'Assomption sashes", named after the Quebec town where many of them were manufactured, were traded throughout much of North America. They were particularly popular with Métis men who worked in the fur trade, and the sash became a symbol of Métis identity.

Northern Ways of Life

"We have a big New Year's dinner on New Year's Night. . . Then, if we've got a gun, we'll sneak out. Right at 12 o'clock–BOOM! We shoot them rifles. Then everybody kisses."

Eric Nystrom, Métis, Rocky Mountain House.

Northern diorama.

Life in the forests and parklands of northern Alberta has always followed a cycle of seasonal change. When people became involved in the fur trade, they added commercial fur trapping, wage labour and trips to the fur trade post to their round of seasonal activities.

Participation in the fur trade meant access to new technologies, new materials and new ways of life. Core values, however, remained intact. People continued a way of life sustained by the land.

New Year's Eve in the North

New Year's was a time of celebration in the north. People outfitted their dog teams in fancy garb and set off to visit neighbours and friends. They welcomed the New Year by firing rifles in the air. Their hosts would come out to greet them and show them where to tie their dogs. Then everyone headed inside to eat and, later, to dance.

Women's Work

Women spent much of their time caring for their families. They looked after children, prepared food, made food and water containers, tanned and smoked hides, and sewed clothing. They also fished, trapped, hunted, and snared birds and small animals. Boredom was seldom a factor. Marie Gallant, a Tsatu Elder, recalls that "the best time in my life was in the bush. Every day there was something to do."

Women took pride in their work. Even everyday objects were well made and designed with an eye to beauty. Spruce root stitching on a birchbark basket was straight and even. Belts were ornamented with richly dyed porcupine quills woven in intricate patterns.

Special care was taken when working with hides. A well-tanned hide was smooth and supple, scraped clean and smoked a warm golden brown before being sewn into jackets, moccasins, gauntlets or pouches.

Hide Tanning

"The process of tanning hides incorporates many elements of nature and individual will. We've always felt that the traditional arts connect a person to his or her environment, taking raw natural resources and transforming them into a unique piece of durable, long-lasting material with no synthetic comparison. It's the bond between the artist and the transformation that appeals to us. It allows us to reflect, to step back to the time of our ancestors, knowing that they once relied on the same materials for their very survival. Our history, it connects us, teaches us who we are, and reminds us of the strength of a people before us.

"Learning the steps involved in tanning hides is relatively easy. It's the technique that becomes challenging and rewarding, realizing that the goal is not the end product but the process. When tanning hides, one is faced with many variables: the seasons, the weather and the changing temperatures–in all, learning what a hide will respond to. Beyond that, it teaches patience, how to be observant, to be responsible, to be prepared and to be resilient.

"For example, the experience of collecting raw materials such as punk spruce for colorant and preserver of hide is a teaching process in itself. It absorbs us into nature by the sights, sounds and smells, and teaches us how nature equalizes, harmonizes and transforms.

"This one craft skill has the ability to guarantee survival not only for an individual but for a culture."

Melissa-Jo and Ben Moses,
Métis and Cree artisans

Sewing roll. Velvet, porcupine quills and hide. Chipewyan. Pre-1919.

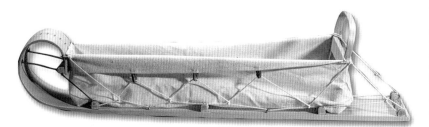

Northern Shelters

Traditional northern shelters were designed to accommodate a mobile way of life. Tipis were the most common form of shelter before the mid-1800s. A conical frame of peeled poles was covered with hides or bark. An opening at the top allowed light to enter and smoke to leave. People packed tipi covers with them when they moved camp and left the poles behind for others to use.

Furnishings were minimal but comfortable. Spruce boughs spread across the floor provided protection from the damp ground. They were replaced every few days, keeping the tipi clean and fragrant. Homemade down blankets, rabbit skin robes and bear and beaver pelts kept people warm.

People built simpler structures when hunting or travelling. A lean-to of hides or brush offered shelter on the trail, and a windbreak of felled spruce trees provided shelter in a pinch.

As they became involved in the fur trade, people began building permanent log dwellings at fur-trade posts and in small river or lakeside settlements. These communities were home bases from which families set out on hunting, trapping and fishing trips.

Once registered trap lines were introduced in the 1930s, many trappers built line cabins along their trap lines. They provided overnight shelter and storage for trapping gear, food and fuel. Like other shelters, cabins were built from materials at hand. Log walls were chinked with moss on the inside and with a mixture of grass and mud or clay on the outside. Dove-tail notching at the cabin's corners (see photo opposite top) made for a tight fit without the use of nails. If glass and metal fixtures were not available, window openings could be covered with parchment-thin hide or flour sacks and door hinges made from moose hide. Today, people use canvas or nylon tents when they travel in the bush.

Top Left:
Snowshoes. Birch wood, babiche, hide and metal nail. Cree or Dene. Circa 1900.

People wear this style of snowshoe when travelling along narrow bush trails and in soft, deep snow.

Above:
Model toboggan. Birch, canvas, imitation sinew and string. Dene Th'a. 1981.

Hitched behind a dog team or a snow machine, a toboggan carries trapping supplies, camp gear and furs. This model, made by Gordon Kotchea of Fort Liard, shows a traditional Dene Th'a style of toboggan, with a high "head", backboard, curved holding bar and canvas wrapper.

Opposite Top Left:
Trappers' log cabin. Inset: Raphael and Louise May Cree in front of their cabin. Cree. Clearwater River. 1977. Courtesy Terry Garvin.

Opposite Centre:
Shot pouch. Common Loon skin and moose hide. Chipewyan or Métis. Circa 1980.

Waterproof pouches made of whole loon skins keep a hunter's shot and powder dry.

Opposite Below:
William Yellowknee uses a drawknife to shape a stretcher. Cree. Chipewyan Lake. 1973.

Animal skins need to be prepared for sale. Animals other than beaver are skinned whole (cased). The skin is turned inside out, the flesh and fat removed, and the cased skin pulled over a stretcher to dry. Stretchers are shaped to an animal's size.

Travel in the North

Survival in the north required mobility. People travelled often and covered great distances. Specialized equipment made of natural materials like hide, wood and bark allowed people to travel across difficult terrain.

Walking was the primary means of travel. People covered hundreds of kilometres on foot each year. Hide moccasins provided comfortable footgear, while snowshoes enabled people to walk through deep snow.

Waterways were major routes of travel year-round. In winter, people walked along frozen rivers and lakes. After spring break-up, they paddled small "rat" canoes through marshes and sloughs while hunting muskrat, beaver and waterfowl. They built larger bark canoes to use on open water and to travel longer distances.

The fur trade changed how people travelled. New means of transport allowed them to cover long distances more quickly and to move heavier loads. Horses, sometimes hitched to wagons, carried people along an established network of trails. People trained dogs to work in teams and to pull toboggans. They built sturdy wooden skiffs to fish and haul supplies. Many men took jobs as boatmen on the large river scows that carried freight to northern fur trade posts.

Everything Comes from the Land

Life in the boreal forest was closely attuned to nature and the changing seasons. In spring, families camped near muskrat trapping grounds and hunted "rats", beaver and migratory waterfowl. Summer and fall were spent hunting moose and caribou, fishing and tanning hides. People put up fish and meat to dry for winter use, collected and dried berries, and made jams and pemmican. Those with gardens harvested crops of potatoes and turnips. Families spent winter trapping fur-bearing animals, hunting game and snaring rabbits.

Children learned bush skills by watching and imitating their parents and grandparents. They acquired an intimate knowledge of animal behaviour, plant habitats and the changing seasons. They also learned the importance of generosity. Successful hunters and fishermen always shared; no one ate while others went hungry.

Animals provided far more than meat. Hides, bones, antlers, organs and sinew were used to make garments, tools, furnishings and other equipment. By making sure that they wasted nothing, people expressed respect–respect for the animals and respect for the Creator whose gifts made life possible.

Hunting Caribou

"When we'd go out for a caribou hunt, we'd go and camp out in the bush. Just kick the snow away and build a fire and put spruce brush for a flooring and that's where we'd camp. Oh boy, sometimes about fifty or sixty below and we got to camp out there, caribou hide for a rug and that's it!

"Then, if we go to hunt from there, we tie up the dogs and sometimes we stay there three or four days, the dogs tied up and we hunt on foot in the bush. Well, nobody goes home until everybody gets their share of meat. So, if I kill five or six caribou and the next guy ten and maybe some guy didn't get any, we share it all up. Nobody comes home with nothing. They all share it up and then they come back to town."

Andrew Campbell, Métis, Fort Chipewyan.

Southern Ways of Life

Right:
Mrs. William Half using a beamer.
Plains Cree. Saddle Lake. 1963.
Courtesy Glenbow Archives, NA-
1433-6.

Hide tanners use beamers to
scrape the hair off smaller and
thinner hides, such as deer.

Left:
Back: Parfleche. Rawhide and
pigments. Siksika. Late 1800s.
Front: Horn spoon and wooden
bowl. Piikani. Late 1800s.

People on the plains and parklands of southern Alberta became involved in the fur trade in different ways than did people in the north. Although they traded buffalo robes and dried meat for European goods, few became trappers. Life remained centred around the buffalo hunt.

People used European materials and technologies to enhance a well-established way of life. They developed complex political systems that co-ordinated the activities of the large numbers of people who now lived together for much of the year. As in the north, this blending of the new with the old shaped a way of life that many people today think of as traditional.

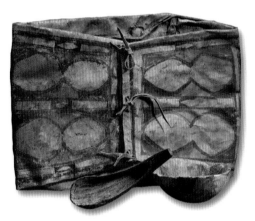

"Real Food"

The Blackfoot called buffalo meat "real food". It was nourishing, tasty and plentiful. Fresh meat usually was served boiled or roasted. When supplies were plentiful, women preserved meat for future use. They sliced it into thin sheets and hung it on drying racks over small, smoky fires. Once it had dried, they packed it in parfleches or pounded it into small bits and mixed it with crushed berries and boiled marrow grease to make pemmican.

Deer, elk, moose and antelope supplemented the buffalo-rich diet. So, too, did prairie turnips and roasted camas bulbs. A soup made of buffalo fat, buffalo blood and berries was a favourite dish at feasts.

Animal products had many other practical uses. Women cut and folded rawhide to make the durable, portable containers called parfleches. Rawhide was used to lash tools together and to make rope, snares and travois lacings. Elk and deer antlers were fashioned into tool handles, and buffalo and mountain sheep horns were shaped into spoons, ladles and powder horns. Animal hair was used as stuffing for pad saddles and braided into rope, bridles and lariats. Berries and pemmican were stored in sacks made from the skins of fetal buffalo calves.

Women's Work

Women's work demanded skill and creativity. Superior work won public admiration and was a source of personal pride. At ceremonies, women described the buffalo robes they had tanned and the garments they had decorated with dyed porcupine quills.

Before they could be made into garments, saddles or pouches, animal hides had to be softened in a process known as tanning. Tanning was hard, time-consuming work. Wet hides were staked to the ground and all the flesh removed. Once the hide had dried, hair was removed with a scraper and the stiff rawhide treated with a mixture of animal brains and fat. The hide was washed in water and stretched, slowly dried over a low fire, and stretched again until it became soft and supple. The entire process took two to three days, with women visiting with each other while they worked.

Hide garments, pouches and other items were often decorated with porcupine quillwork. As glass trade beads began replacing porcupine quills, quillwork sometimes became a specialized and sacred art. Blackfoot quill workers prayed for endurance and painted their faces and hands to protect them from blindness and swelling. A novice quill worker offered her first completed project as a gift to the Sun.

Their Own Boss: The Plains Métis

By the mid-1800s, Métis on the plains of southern Alberta had developed a distinctive way of life as independent traders, settlers, trappers and buffalo hunters. The Cree called these independent people Otipimisowak, or "their own boss".

The merger of the North West and Hudson's Bay companies in 1821 signalled the end of an era for many Métis fur trade employees. Released from their contracts, they established small settlements in the lake country of central Alberta and supported themselves and their families by fishing, hunting, farming, trapping and freighting.

The growing settlements quickly attracted new members. Hudson's Bay Company traders set up posts and stores, and missionaries built churches and schools. By the 1870s, settlements like Lac Ste. Anne, St. Albert and Victoria Settlement (Pakan) had become home to many Métis.

The buffalo hunt marked the high point of the year. Each summer and fall, families loaded up their Red River carts and headed for the plains. They travelled in large brigades supervised by a hunt leader, captains, guides and soldiers. Tight discipline protected the brigades from attack and made sure the hunt proceeded in an orderly fashion.

While most families returned home after the hunt, some stayed behind in log cabin settlements. These winterers, or hivernants, spent the winter hunting buffalo and processing hides into robes destined for sale on international markets.

Materials excavated at Buffalo Lake, an hivernant settlement in central Alberta, show how the Plains Métis drew on Aboriginal and European traditions to create their own distinctive culture. People at Buffalo Lake wore tailored cloth garments and made hide moccasins and gauntlets. They hunted on horseback but shod their horses. They used traditional healing methods alongside patent medicines, ate pemmican with canned fruit, and poured tea from fine china services.

Top:
"Half Breeds Travelling." Paul Kane. 1846. Courtesy Royal Ontario Museum.

Above:
Ceramic sherd in "Ivy" pattern, dinner fork and teaspoon. Métis. 1870s. Excavated at Buffalo Lake.

Tipi furnishings were both practical and decorative. Willow backrests supported by wooden tripods provided comfortable seating and were easily packed when moving camp. Beds were made from bundles of dried grass covered with buffalo robes and blankets. Baby swings, pouches and weapons were draped from tipi poles and tripods, while clothing and food provisions were stored in parfleches stashed behind backrests.

Although Aboriginal people have lived in houses for more than a century, they continue to make and use tipis. Tipis are popular shelters at powwows and other social gatherings and are the most suitable setting for many ceremonies.

Tipi as Home

Tipis were comfortable, practical and attractive homes. Ingenious engineering kept them warm in winter and cool in summer. Easily transported and quickly assembled, they made ideal dwellings for mobile people.

A sophisticated design perfected over thousands of years made the tipi energy-efficient. A stone-lined firepit heated the entire tipi yet consumed little fuel. Adjustable smoke flaps regulated drafts and directed smoke out of the tipi. Liners tied to tipi poles helped maintain the upward flow of air and provided effective insulation against spring rains, summer sun and winter cold. They also brought privacy, catching the shadows cast by the fire before they could be projected against the tipi wall.

Until the late 1800s, tipi covers were made of unsmoked, tanned buffalo hides sewn together with sinew. An exceptionally large tipi required as many as thirty hides, but ten to fourteen hides were the norm. After the buffalo disappeared from the Alberta Plains in the 1870s, women made tipi covers out of canvas.

A Blackfoot Weasel Tail Suit Transfer Ceremony

The scene below depicts a transfer ceremony held at Sundance Flats in southern Alberta. A young boy has just received a weasel tail suit, a distinctive outfit named for the white weasel pelt fringes on both shirt and leggings.

Weasel tail suits are medicine bundles or items with special spiritual significance. They have their own face paint and songs and must be transferred by a person who has the rights to the bundle in a ceremony like the one shown here.

The first weasel tail suit was a gift from the Sun to Scarface, the hero who helped bring the Sun Dance to the Blackfoot. It protected him against illness and helped him reach old age. The large discs on the shirtfront represent the Sun, and the suit transfer ceremony is often held at the annual Sun Dance. The ceremony marks the boy's initiation into Blackfoot ceremonial life.

The ceremony depicted in the diorama shown below is accompanied by a giveaway in which the boy's relatives distribute gifts to the guests they have invited. They are giving the man who conducted the ceremony a fully outfitted team of horses. These gifts express the family's support for the boy and announce that he has become a person worthy of community respect. They also confirm the family's status as "people of plenty"— wealthy, successful and generous.

Giveaway diorama.

Spiritual Life

"Everything is Spirit. The reason things live is because they have Spirit. When you remove the Spirit, they die."

Gordon Rain, Plains Cree Elder,
Louis Bull First Nation.

Right:
Wolf Collar's Thunder Shield. Rawhide, flicker feathers, glass beads, hair, pigments, wood and brass bell. Siksika. Circa 1875.

Everything is Spirit

Spirit is everywhere and influences all aspects of life. People receive sacred blessings when they approach the Spirits with reverence and respect or when the Spirits come to them.

Sky, Land and Water are all infused with Spirit. Sun brings food, air and light. Thunder, with his flapping wings and flashing eyes, sends thunderbolts crashing across the sky. Fertile spring rains soon follow. Land and Water Spirits live in the rocks and trees, in rivers and lakes, and in animals. They supply food, clothing and shelter. Each Spirit also offers its own special blessing–strength, courage or long life.

People receive sacred blessings through prayer, ceremony and spiritual encounters. Spirit helpers, often animals who appear in human form, come to people in visions and dreams. They teach them their power songs and explain how to make and care for sacred objects.

In the early 1900s, the Siksika healer Wolf Collar recalled an early encounter with a Spirit helper.

"When I was seventeen, a strange thing happened to me. About noon, Thunder struck me in the teeth and on the left arm and side. I lay there until sunset. Thunder gave me a tipi and a shield. She told me to fear nothing and that I would become an old man."

Wolf Collar. From *The North American Indian,* by Edward Curtis.

A Thunder Shield, a Painted Yellow Otter Tipi, a lizard amulet–each originated in a vision or dream, and each embodies the power of a spiritual helper. If properly cared for and sustained by daily prayer, these personal medicines provide assistance throughout life.

Earth:
Realm
of the
Real People

Spirit World:
Realm of the Spirits

Night Sky:
Realm of the
Above People

Otter's trail   Highlighted throats
and kidneys represent
the sources of Otter's
spiritual power

Guardian Spirits and Dusty Stars

On the northern Plains, tipi designs are complex and highly symbolic. They depict guardian spirits, constellations of stars, and vision quest sites in nearby hills and mountains. Each tipi design has its own set of stories, songs and sacred objects.

Designs originate in dreams and visions. Otters, serpents, buffalo and other animals painted on tipi covers represent spiritual guardians who have answered a vision-seeker's prayers for spiritual power. They show the vision-seeker how to paint his tipi and teach him sacred songs and rites.

Blackfoot tipi covers place these spirits in a symbolic landscape. At the tipi top, brilliant constellations dance against the nighttime sky. The band of earth encircling the tipi base is punctuated by rounded hills or pointed peaks and by "dusty stars"–prairie puffballs formed when meteors fell to earth.

Stories link these designs with characters and episodes from oral tradition–with the lost children who found a new home in the Pleiades, the slain hero Blood Clot whose blood turned the rocks red, or the hilltop sites where people fast and receive their visions. A painted tipi recreates a world at once deeply familiar and profoundly spiritual.

Smudging and Purification

People smudge to purify themselves before gatherings where prayers are offered or spiritual matters discussed. They purify themselves before handling sacred objects, and the objects themselves are smudged before being used in a ceremony. People also smudge to cleanse the atmosphere after something negative has happened. A smudge removes harmful influences and restores harmony.

Special containers called smudge boxes hold live coals and smouldering material. Sweetgrass, picked while it is green and plaited into long braids, is often used in smudging. Dry sweetgrass may be broken off and dropped on coals or hot stones to make the smudge, or the braid itself may be burned. People also smudge with tree fungus, sweetpine and sage.

As the burning substance releases fragrant incense, people direct the smoke over their body to prepare themselves for prayer. Smoke carries their prayers upwards to the Creator and the spirit world.

Left:
Yellow Painted Otter tipi design. The three otters facing the left are female, the three otters facing right are male; the ochre colored scalloped edge represents the foothills; the circles below represent Dusty Stars or Prairie Puffballs (meteors); the seven circles on the top left represent the Seven Brothers (The Big Dipper); the six circles on the top right represent The Lost Children (The Pleiades); the black stripe represents The Otter's Trail or Thunder/Sun Dogs.

Above:
Smudge box with a braid of sweetgrass. 1997.

Personal Bundles

Personal bundles contain sacred items associated with an individual's spirit helper. Most bundles have one or more songs associated with them. Bundles, songs and the spirit's protective power can be transferred from one person to another in a transfer ceremony.

Amulets are the smallest kind of personal bundle. They are worn in the hair, around the neck or attached to clothing. One special type of amulet made by northern Plains nations holds a child's navel cord. A mother, grandmother or aunt wraps a newborn infant's cord with sweetgrass, sweetpine or a pinch of tobacco and sews it into a small hide pouch. The pouch is made in the shape of a lizard, turtle or snake. During the baby's earliest years, the amulet is fastened to the front of her cradle. When she grows old enough to walk, it can be attached to her clothing or worn around her neck.

The choice of animal varies among First Nations. Both Nakoda and Blackfoot girls, however, wear amulets representing the lizard, while boys wear snake amulets. These animals are believed to enjoy long and healthy lives, and their spirit helps protect children from illness. Their shedding skin also parallels the changes children experience as they pass through life's stages. In the amulet shown to the left, the cord was sewn inside the tube that forms the snake's body. The attached pouch held tobacco.

Above:
T-shaped pipe: Catlinite, wood, silk ribbon, porcupine quills, mallard skin and horsehair. Plains. Circa 1890. Tobacco cutting board: wood and brass-plated iron tacks. Kainai. Late 1800s. Bearberry leaves: dried and crushed bearberry leaves and cloth. Kainai. Mid-1900s.

Lower Right:
Girl's amulet. Hide, glass beads and sinew. Nakoda. Late 1800s.

Below:
Boy's amulet. Hide and glass beads. Nakoda. Early 1900s.

Connecting Heart and Mind: The Pipe

"The Pipe opens the connection between heart and mind. It carries your message when you're trying to connect with the spiritual world. It's a tool for making a connection with the Creator."

Raven Makkannaw, Plains Cree Elder.

Pipe smoking starts many significant events, from a meeting to discuss community affairs to the opening of a sacred bundle. People also smoke pipes to seal agreements and solidify alliances. The smoke carries a message to the spirit world, asking the Creator and the spirits to hear prayers.

Ceremonial smoking follows a set protocol. People sit in a circle and pass the pipe clockwise, following the direction the sun travels across the sky. Accepting the pipe indicates a willingness to discuss an issue and a promise to speak truthfully.

Many people have private pipes for everyday use. These, too, are handled with respect. They are well cared for and often carried in ornamented pipe bags.

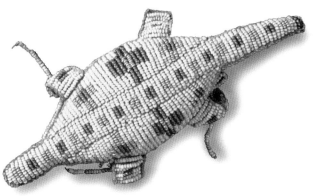

The Healing Spirit

Herbal remedies provide relief for many common ailments, including colds and headaches. More serious illnesses require treatment by specialists. People may consult western doctors, but they also use traditional healers.

Traditional healers prepare medicinal teas and pastes from a variety of plant and animal materials. These medicines activate the body's natural ability to heal. Other healing techniques include bloodletting and removing intrusive objects. Many treatments require combinations of different roots, barks and leaves.

Traditional healing involves more than mixing herbs or letting blood. It requires faith, respect and prayer. Spirit helpers play an essential role, guiding the healer and strengthening the herbs' potency.

Above:
Healer's rattle. Rawhide, wood, weasel tails and chrome-plated brass bells. Piikani? Early 1900s.

Healers may use rattles to call for assistance from spirit helpers and to drive away the forces that cause illness.

Left:
Medicine root scraper. Wood, tin and nails. Plains Cree. Late 1800s.

The Cree Sun Dance

Cree spirituality emphasizes harmony between people and nature. It recognizes that harmony sometimes can only be achieved through struggle and self-sacrifice. These themes come to the forefront in the Sun Dance, the major ceremonial event in Plains Cree spiritual life. It is held in late spring, a time of renewal, and brings people from different communities together in prayer, thanksgiving and celebration.

Preparations get underway in winter, when a man of solid spiritual standing vows to make a Sun Dance. He may be inspired by a desire to assist someone who is ill or by advice from a spirit. Over the following months, he holds a series of preliminary ceremonies, avoids alcohol, shuns conflict and prays daily. When the time arrives, he supervises construction of the Sun Dance Lodge and the raising of the centre pole.

The Lodge is a sacred structure that recreates the world in microcosm. The centre pole anchors the Lodge to the earth and carries prayers upwards to the sky. Coloured cloths are tied to the centre pole and rafters as offerings to the spirits. Inside the Lodge, celebrants sing Sun Dance songs and present offerings to the spirit world in thanks for past assistance. They go without food or drink to cleanse themselves spiritually. As they dance, they pray for the recovery of the sick, the resolution of personal troubles, and the well being of all the people.

Below:
"Sun Dance on the Reserve". Allen Sapp. 1992. Courtesy Allen Sapp.

Okan: The Blackfoot Sun Dance

Okan is the great ceremonial event of the Blackfoot year. It is held at the height of summer, when people traditionally gathered for a communal buffalo hunt. It brings the community together in prayer and celebration.

Preparations begin when a virtuous woman calls upon the Sun to intercede in a life crisis. She publicly vows to sponsor the Sun Dance and to acquire the Natoas, or Sun Dance bundle. It contains the objects she will need to carry out her duties as Holy Woman.

Okan is a complex series of ceremonies in which prayer forms the common link. Okan is rooted in stories of legendary figures like Soatsaki (Woman Who Married a Star) and Scarface. Soatsaki brought the Natoas bundle to her people by descending to Earth through a hole in the sky created when she dug up a sacred turnip. The turnip and digging stick are key elements of the Natoas bundle, while the hide ropes that tie together the rafters of the Holy Woman's Lodge represent the ropes that lowered Soatsaki to Earth. Another story tells how Soatsaki's son, Scarface, killed seven giant cranes that threatened the life of his father, Morning Star. Scarface presented the heads as an offering to his grandparents, Sun and Moon. In gratitude for having saved Morning Star's life, Sun made Scarface his messenger to the Blackfoot. Sun promised to safeguard the people's well-being if they held a Sun Dance in his honour each year, and he taught Scarface the Sun Dance songs, prayers and protocol.

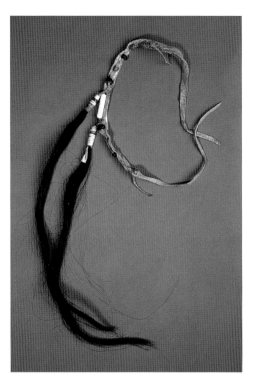

Just as these female and male figures contributed different elements to the Sun Dance, so too do women and men play complementary roles. The Holy Woman presides over the Natoas bundle and the offering of boiled buffalo tongues. Her husband sings buffalo songs. Weather dancers, men who communicate with the spirits, fast, pray and dance in the Sun Dance Lodge.

Dene Spirituality

Most Dene encounter the Spirit world through stories, dreams and visions. A few go further, developing the ability to control their dreams. They are the prophets who look into the future. They dream for their people.

When dreaming or in a trance, prophets travel to heaven, where they are met by ancestral Spirits, or "angels". The Spirits give them drum songs, flag designs and knowledge of the future. Prophets use this knowledge to help people find game, plan for a cold winter or prepare for hard times.

In the early 1900s, the Dene Th'a prophet Nogha foresaw troubling changes for his people. Oil-field development, government checks and settlement on reserves would threaten their established way of life. People would live behind fences, game would disappear and children and parents would grow apart. Nogha tried to prepare the Dene Th'a to cope with these radical changes. He warned them to avoid alcohol and urged them to pray, sing and hold Tea Dances.

The Dene Th'a Tea Dance brings communities together in a circle of prayer. The circle embraces the ancestors, whose spirits are called on to help with prayers. It embraces the Creator, to whom offerings of tea, tobacco and moose fat are made. And it embraces the young people, for whom special prayers are given.

Métis and Spirituality

Métis draw strength from the spiritual ways of both their First Nations and European ancestors. Some find spiritual sustenance in the Tea Dance, Sun Dance or sweatlodge. For others, Catholic mass, Anglican communion and Christian prayer provide the framework for spiritual life.

Many Métis weave elements of First Nations and Christian spirituality together. Parishioners may decorate their local church with sweetgrass in place of palms on Palm Sunday. After a funeral mass, family members may leave a meal or some tobacco on the deceased's grave as an offering to the ancestors. A prayer may be accompanied by both a smudge and the rosary. Reverence for "a spirit within" provides the common link between different spiritual traditions.

Above:
Smudge and rosary. Wihkomasokan (fungus), iron, tin-plated copper, plastic and paint. Métis. 1990s.

Left:
Tea Dance drum and beater. Deer rawhide, birch, aspen, maple, babiche, acetate ribbon and cotton cord. Dene Th'a. 1997.

Drumbeats mark footsteps along the path to the Spirit world. This drum was made for the Gallery by Jean Pastion of Chateh, Alberta.

In All Their Finery

The Museum's Aboriginal collections include a number of objects of exceptional beauty. Some of these are featured in a portion of the gallery called "In All Their Finery". Although displayed as fine-art pieces, these objects were also designed for practical use. The artistry involved in their creation, the skilful use of materials, and the symbolism embedded in the designs speak to the intertwining of the spiritual and the everyday that is an essential component of Aboriginal world view. Following is a selection of some of these fine objects.

Top Left: with detail
Man's jacket. Moose hide, silk thread, beaver fur and porcupine quills. Cree or Dene. Pre-1930. Moccasins. Moose hide and silk thread. Cree or Métis. Pre-1914. Gauntlets. Moose hide, silk thread, fur and cloth. Métis. Pre-1914.

Lower Left:
Pouch. Swan, mallard and other waterfowl pelts. Dene. Late 1800s.

Right:
Panel bag. Wool, glass and brass beads, ribbon and cotton cloth. Cree or Métis. Mid-1800s.

Top: with detail
Baby belt. Caribou hide, porcupine quills, crane bones and glass beads. Dene Th'a. 1940. Made and used by Adeline Sibbertson Semper as a sling to carry her children.

Left and Below: with detail
Frock coat. Caribou hide, porcupine quills and cotton. Métis. Mid-1800s.

Above:
Headdress with trailer. Bald and golden eagle feathers, felt, wool, ribbon, weasel pelts, human hair, glass beads, hide and buttons. Nakoda. Pre-1917.

Above Right:
Horse mask. Canvas, hide, glass beads and thread. Tsuu T'ina. Pre-1919.

Lower Right:
Cradle. Hide, glass beads, cowrie shells, velvet, wool, cotton fabric, metal and brass tacks, metal screws and cardboard. Nakoda. Circa 1917.

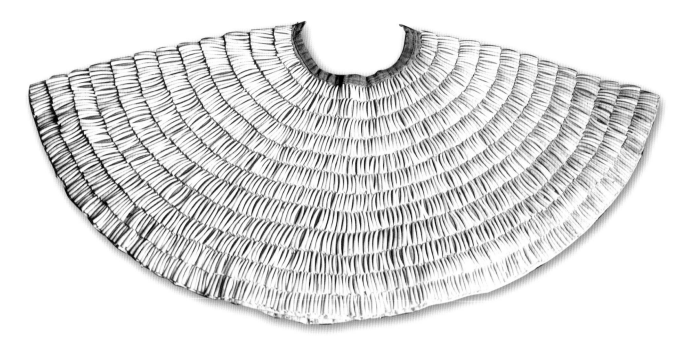

Above:
Woman's cape. Dentalia shells, cotton sateen and cotton muslin. Blackfoot? Circa 1890.

Left:
Woman's dress. Wool, ribbon, cowrie shells, glass "basket" beads, hawk bells and thimbles. Blackfoot. Late 1800s.

Suppression and Resistance

"The Dominion has purchased the whole of the North-West, and it belongs to Canada."
Prime Minister John A. Macdonald, 1875.

The Dominion of Canada purchased title to the Northwest from the Hudson's Bay Company in 1870. Overnight, Aboriginal peoples' homeland became Canada's frontier. Eleven treaties were signed between 1871 and 1921. They extinguished First Nations title to most of northwestern Canada, including Alberta, and assigned First Nations people to Indian reserves. Métis title was extinguished by the provision of scrip.

Much of what constituted Native identity would be destroyed during the following century of cultural suppression and change. But much would survive, as Aboriginal people continued to place their confidence in the enduring practices that had always sustained them.

The Manitou Stone

The Manitou Stone is sacred to the Aboriginal people of central Alberta and Saskatchewan. It is credited with having protected the great buffalo herds that sustained human life and with inspiring reverence and peace among different nations.

The Manitou Stone is a meteorite, a solid piece of iron that fell from the sky onto the plains of eastern Alberta. Saulteaux tradition says that it was placed on a hill overlooking Iron Creek by the Great Spirit or Manitou.

In the spring of 1866, Methodist missionaries loaded the Manitou Stone onto a cart and took it to their mission at Victoria Settlement. Aboriginal spiritual leaders prophesied that war, plague and famine would follow.

In 1869, warfare broke out between the Plains Cree and Blackfoot. Before it was over, more than 400 people had died. The following year, smallpox swept the countryside. It claimed over 3500 lives. Hundreds more died of starvation that winter when the buffalo failed to come north. The terrible prophecy had been fulfilled.

Killing Off the Buffalo

Some forty million buffalo still roamed the North American plains in the 1830s. But their numbers were decreasing with each passing year. In the fall of 1878, the last remnants of the once-great herds crossed south into Montana. They never returned.

The fur trade had taken a heavy toll. For decades commercial hunters, both Aboriginal and non-Aboriginal, had supplied the trade with huge quantities of pemmican and buffalo robes. After 1870, a growing demand for leather in eastern tanneries fuelled a booming trade in buffalo hides. Under such sustained pressure, the buffalo population steadily fell.

The situation became desperate in the 1870s when the U.S. government launched a campaign to exterminate the buffalo. Determined to break Native American resistance to western settlement, the Army hired hunters to eradicate the animals on which the people depended for survival. Since buffalo moved freely across the international border, slaughter in the U.S. meant fewer animals in Canada.

Some Aboriginal leaders tried to avert the coming disaster. They urged the government to implement conservation measures to protect the remaining herds. An ordinance passed in 1877 proved ineffective. In any case, it was too little too late. The Plains buffalo were gone.

A market in discarded buffalo bones thrived for several years after the buffalo had disappeared from the Canadian Plains. Buffalo horns, hooves and bones were collected in carts, loaded onto rail cars and freighted to eastern factories. There they were ground into powder and made into fertilizer and carbon for refining sugar.

Canada's National Policy

Canada moved quickly to consolidate its hold over its new territories. In 1873, a paramilitary force was established to bring the Northwest under the rule of Canadian law. The North West Mounted Police shut down the illegal whiskey trade from the United States and patrolled the international border. They also supervised the relocation of Aboriginal people to reserves.

In 1879, surveyors arrived in Alberta to assess farming and ranching prospects and to evaluate mineral, oil and timber resources. They laid out a rigid grid of townships, sections and quarter sections, preparing the land for homesteading. The completion of a transcontinental rail line in 1885 provided the final link in the expanding national economy. It brought immigrants and manufactured goods west and carried wheat and livestock back to eastern markets. It also made possible the large-scale commercial exploitation of natural resources.

This infrastructure in place, the Department of the Interior launched a campaign in 1896 to promote immigration. Overseas recruitment drives, aggressive advertising, and the offer of free 160-acre homesteads attracted thousands of new settlers. By 1911, Aboriginal people counted for fewer than 5 percent of Alberta's population.

Below:
Colorado settlers arriving by special train in Bassano, Alberta. 1914. Courtesy Glenbow Archives NA 984-2.

Lower Right:
Mound of buffalo skulls at the Michigan Carbon Works, Detroit, 1880. Courtesy Detroit Public Library.

Lower Left:
Immigration recruitment poster. 1910-1920. Courtesy Glenbow Archives NA 5580-1.

Treaty

Aboriginal people had long used treaties to settle disputes and forge alliances. Leaders drew on this experience when federal government representatives arrived to negotiate treaties. On the Plains and parklands, the chiefs and headmen who signed Treaty Six and Treaty Seven secured promises of farm equipment, livestock, education and medical care. Chief Poundmaker took a hard line with the Treaty Six commissioners. "This is our land!" he told them. "It isn't a piece of pemmican to be cut off and given in little pieces back to us. It is ours and we will take what we want." His firm stance helped win promises of health care, farming assistance, and famine relief. In the north, the leaders who signed Treaty Eight obtained assurances that traditional hunting, fishing and trapping rights would be protected and spiritual practices respected. These promises were to hold "as long as the sun shines and the waters flow."

Participants came away with different understandings of what had been agreed upon. Treaty commissioners asserted that Aboriginal people had "ceded forever" their claim to land in exchange for reserves and limited assistance. But Aboriginal people considered the treaties an alliance among sovereign nations. They had not surrendered their land. They had agreed to share it in return for help in building a new way of life.

Treaties marked the beginning of a relationship in which the British monarch and the federal government committed themselves to lasting responsibilities towards First Nations. Treaties linked Canadians, Aboriginal and non-Aboriginal, together in an enduring relationship of mutual obligation and shared destiny. Promises would be broken over the coming years, but the underlying relationship, with its guarantees of rights recognized under treaty, would endure.

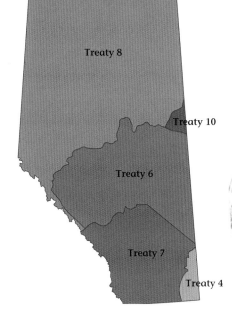

Treaty 8
Treaty 10
Treaty 6
Treaty 7
Treaty 4

The Spirit and Intent of Treaty Six

"I know that in Treaty Six, the Elders before me drilled these ideas about the Treaty and how they understood it into us. They told us repeatedly that the written text is not what our people agreed to.

"First of all, the people were aware that the white man was going to arrive eventually into their territory. They were also quite aware that the buffalo was disappearing. They were aware that their lifestyle as far as their reliance on the buffalo for their survival was coming to an end. So in 1876, when the Treaty was signed, the Cree people saw the Treaty as a means for their survival. They saw it as an agreement between two people to co-exist, for our people to maintain what they had always had. They agreed to share the land with the newcomer and that the government would provide them with medicine and education so that they could learn how to make a living in this new society. . .

"[They saw it as] a sacred agreement between our people and the Crown, now the right of Canada, made in the name of the Creator."

Ki'sikaw Ksay-yin, Plains Cree,
Ermineskin Band.

The Indian Act: Policies for Assimilation

"I want to get rid of the Indian problem . . . Our object is to continue until there is not a single Indian in Canada that has not been absorbed into the body politic, and there is no Indian question, and no Indian Department . . ."

Duncan Campbell Scott,
Deputy Superintendent-General of Indian
Affairs. 1920.

In 1867, the British North America Act transferred responsibility for "Indians and Lands Reserved for Indians" from the British Crown to the Dominion of Canada. Parliament spelled out the terms under which it would exercise this responsibility when it passed the first Canadian Indian Act in 1876.

The Indian Act was designed to protect Indian people until they could be assimilated into mainstream Euro-Canadian society. In the interim, it made Indians wards of the state, with a legal status equivalent to that of children. They were denied such fundamental rights as the vote in federal elections and the right to dispose of their own property.

Restructuring almost every aspect of Aboriginal life, the Indian Act legally defined who was and who was not an Indian. It determined who could and who could not live on reserves. Non-Indians were considered trespassers if they lived on reserve without the Indian agent's permission. The policy even applied to status women who married non-status men. They and their children were excluded from band membership, had no Treaty rights and could only live on reserves if they had a licence from the Indian agent.

Top:
Chief's Treaty Seven jacket, hat, scarf and belt. Worsted wool, rayon ribbon, brass buttons, wool felt, viscose, leather and brass. Kainai. Mid-1900s.

Above:
Treaty card pouch. Hide, glass beads, brass beads, bone pipe beads, cowrie shells, conch shells and wool stroud. Plains Cree. Circa 1880s.

People produced treaty cards at treaty payment time as proof of eligibility to receive annuities. Some individuals carried their cards in decorated pouches.

Right:
Sir Cecil Edward Denny. Denny acted as the Indian Agent for all Treaty Seven First Nations from 1882-83. Circa 1912. Courtesy Glenbow Institute NA-1847-4.

The Indian Agent

"Everything had to go through the administration of the government. The Indian agent, he was the almighty. If you had to go to town you had to get a permit . . . If you had cattle that you wanted to sell, you had to get a permit. You couldn't slaughter your own animals. You had to get a piece of paper stating you had the right to do these things. Our people found it very ridiculous and it hurt us in our hearts."

Raven Makkannaw, Plains Cree Elder.

A new political system of elected band chiefs and councils was also imposed by the Indian Act. This system was designed to replace traditional political structures with Euro-Canadian political institutions. Treaties stipulated that band chiefs and counsellors receive European-style treaty suits. Despite this show of respect, the Indian Act allowed band councils limited authority. Indian agents could remove from office chiefs whom they considered unsuitable and overrule band council decisions with which they disagreed. Some bands refused to hold elections and continued to honour traditional leaders. Others simply elected as chiefs traditional leaders already in power.

When Aboriginal people resisted the government's program of directed change, the Act was amended to increase government powers and hasten assimilation goals. Some amendments targeted traditional spiritual practices. Others imposed a new system of education, a new political structure, and new forms of family life. The Indian Act has been amended and revised many times since 1876. But it still remains in effect.

Indian agents administered the Indian Act. It gave them enormous discretionary control over virtually every aspect of day-to-day life in Indian communities. Agents managed band funds and oversaw economic ventures. They acted as justices of the peace and had the power to both prosecute and sentence Indians accused of violating the Indian Act.

Indian agents not only managed a community's official business, they oversaw residents' personal affairs. They issued food rations, supervised farm operations, enforced school attendance, assigned housing and settled domestic disputes. They had the authority to withhold rations and to issue passes that allowed people to leave their reserves temporarily.

Some Indian agents worked hard to benefit the communities to which they had been assigned. But others used coercive tactics to push forward policies that worked against communities' interests. In 1917-18, for example, the Blood Indian agent forced a vote on the surrender of a large tract of reserve land. He denied those who voted against the surrender permission to withdraw money from their personal accounts and gave individuals who favoured the sale cash advances against future earnings. The proposal passed by a small margin but was overturned when charges of bribery and fraud were raised.

By 1969, all Indian agents had been removed from office as First Nations moved toward self-determination.

Riel's Resistance

1885 was a time of crisis in the Northwest. The Métis had sent dozens of petitions to Ottawa requesting resolution of their outstanding land claims. Not one had been answered. Now surveyors were headed west, paving the way for white settlement. Alarmed, Métis in Saskatchewan formed a provisional government under the leadership of Louis Riel, the man who had won a land base for the Manitoba Métis fifteen years before. When they heard that a police force had been sent to arrest Riel and disband their government, the Métis raised their own army and called on Indian allies for support.

Indians faced a different set of issues. For many bands, survival itself was at stake. The buffalo were gone, farm programs were collapsing and rations had been slashed. Concerned leaders had tried to improve conditions through protests and petitions. In 1883, nine Edmonton-area chiefs sent a petition to Prime Minister Macdonald complaining that insufficient farm equipment and cattle, coupled with a new "work for rations" policy, violated promises made during the Treaty Six negotiations. They called on the government to honour its treaty commitments and provide aid for their starving people. When their letter was read on the floor of the House of Commons, though, Macdonald dismissed it as the work of inveterate complainers. "The Indians will always grumble", he proclaimed; "they will never profess to be satisfied."

Matters came to a head in March, when North West Mounted Police and Métis forces clashed at Duck Lake, Saskatchewan. Ottawa dispatched over 5000 troops to suppress the resistance and depose Riel. Several battles were fought over the following weeks. Each time, attacking government militia were forced to retreat. Superior numbers and artillery finally broke the resistance on May 12, when Canadian troops took the Métis capital, Batoche.

Reprisals were harsh. Riel was executed and his counsellors thrown in jail. Branded rebels and traitors, many of the Métis who had participated in the resistance moved west to Alberta, hoping to build a new life.

Most Indian bands avoided the conflict. Although disappointed with the government, the chiefs had agreed to uphold peace when they signed Treaty and

Above:
Big Bear (Left) and Poundmaker (Right). 1886. Courtesy Glenbow Archives NA-1315-18.

Right:
Musket, ram rod, powder horn and shot pouch. Metal, wood, cow horn, hide and sinew. Nakoda/Plains Cree. Circa 1885.

Poundmaker's brother, Yellow Mud Blanket, used this equipment at Cut Knife Hill. The firearm is a British-made Hollis & Sons musket.

they were determined to honour their commitment. Plains Cree and Nakoda Chiefs Muddy Bull and Sharphead, for example, assured Indian Commissioner Edgar Dewdney that, "[we will] have nothing to do with the insurgents and . . . [will] remain loyal till death."

A few Saskatchewan bands, however, were drawn into battle. Poundmaker's band became involved when Canadian troops attacked their camp at Cut Knife Hill; Big Bear's band was involved in an attack on the Indian agency at Frog Lake, Alberta, that left nine white men dead. In each instance, the Chief intervened to prevent further loss of life. Poundmaker interceded with the war Chief Fine Day to stop his warriors from firing on retreating government troops, and Big Bear protected the lives of individuals taken captive at

Frog Lake. But the public perception was that the chiefs had encouraged their followers to take up arms against the government. Like Riel, they were put on trial and convicted of treason.

Although Indian involvement had been limited, the government enacted a series of repressive post-resistance measures that applied to all bands. It confiscated rifles and handguns, curtailed ammunition sales and implemented a new pass system that turned reserves into places of confinement. Poundmaker, Big Bear and twenty-one others were imprisoned, eight warriors executed, and Big Bear's band dispersed. Many members fled across the border to Montana. Big Bear spoke for many when he said, "My heart is on the ground."

Taking Scrip

"The halfbreeds . . . are whites [and should be treated] as if they were altogether white."

Prime Minister John A. Macdonald. 1885.

For the Métis, being treated "as if they were altogether white" meant no treaties, no reserves, no special hunting or trapping rights and no promises of economic or medical help. They did, however, have claims to land. Unhappiness over the government's failure to address these claims had helped spark Riel's Resistance. In March 1885, less than two weeks after the formation of Riel's provisional government, Ottawa appointed a Royal Commission to settle these claims. Over the next three years, commissioners travelled throughout central and southern Alberta issuing certificates known as scrip. The government continued to use the scrip process to extinguish Métis title to lands covered by subsequent treaties. A commission formed in 1899 issued scrip to northern Métis living in the area covered by the newly signed Treaty Eight.

Heads of families were asked to choose between land scrip, redeemable in Crown land, and money scrip, redeemable in cash. Most people chose money scrip. It seemed a practical choice at the time, particularly for those who supported their families by hunting and trapping, but its long-term result–landlessness–would prove devastating. Métis in St. Albert were among the few to choose land scrip. They used it to secure title to homesteads that they had already developed. Some of those who took land scrip, however, later lost their homes when they were unable to pay property taxes.

Almost as devastating was the fraud that riddled the scrip program. Speculators bought up certificates the moment they were issued. They persuaded Métis to sign over powers of attorney, bribed individuals to impersonate scrip applicants, and

purchased certificates at less than one-third of face value. Speculators quickly acquired over 95 percent of the 1.1 million acres intended for Alberta Métis.

Top:
Money scrip. 1885. Courtesy Provincial Archives of Alberta 82.107/7.

Above:
Land scrip. 1898. Courtesy Glenbow Archives NA-2839-5.

Winning Souls for Christ

Missionary work in Alberta got underway in 1840 when Wesleyan Methodist Robert Rundle was appointed chaplain to the Hudson's Bay Company at Fort Edmonton. Over the next eight years, Rundle travelled throughout central Alberta, baptizing new converts, performing Christian marriages and conducting open-air services in Cree and Nakoda camps. Two years after Rundle's arrival, the Roman Catholic church established a mission west of Fort Edmonton at Lac Ste. Anne. Over the coming decades, rival Protestant and Catholic churches would build a series of Christian institutions–mission schools, farms, hospitals and orphanages–throughout the Northwest.

At first, many Aboriginal people welcomed missionaries. They accepted them as individuals with access to spiritual power and were willing to adopt beliefs and practices that were compatible with their own. But missionaries brought more than the good news of salvation. Confident that they were serving the cause of progress, they promoted a way of life based on European values and assumptions. They warned children to stay away from so-called pagan ceremonies. Some went so far as to destroy sacred objects and confiscate bundles.

Missionaries tried to prepare people for changes they believed were inevitable. But they were themselves agents of change. As Methodist missionary John Maclean put it, "[C]ivilizing the Indian race ... implies the full transformation and development of the nature of the individual, the complete overthrow of religious, political and social customs, and very many changes in the domestic relations of the people." In their quest to win souls for Christ, missionaries altered the sacred balance of life.

Outlawing Spirituality

"Every Indian or other person who engages in . . . any Indian festival, dance or other ceremony of which the giving away or paying or giving back of money, goods, or articles of any sort forms a part . . . and every Indian or other person who engages or assists in any celebration or dance of which the wounding or mutilation of the dead or living body of any human being or animal forms a part … is guilty of an indictable offence."

Section 114 of the Indian Act,
as amended in 1895.

In the late 1800s, government officials and missionaries launched a campaign to suppress traditional spirituality. Denouncing dancing, drumming and singing as "foolish amusements" or acts of "devil worship", they complained that sacred ceremonies were preventing Aboriginal people from assimilating into Canadian society.

Officials singled out giveaways and the Sun Dance piercing ritual for special condemnation. In their eyes, piercing was considered a barbaric warrior's ritual, while giveaways discouraged individual initiative and respect for private property. The Sun Dance itself was not prohibited, but officials did their best to suppress it. Bands had to request permission to hold Sun Dances; most requests were denied. Those ceremonies that did take place were often held under the watchful eye of the North West Mounted Police. Traditional healers also came under attack. They could be arrested if they accepted payment for healing and had to conduct their medicinal practices in secret.

The official campaign to suppress spirituality ended in 1951 with the removal of regulations banning ceremonial practices from the newly revised Indian Act. Over the years, some communities had secretly defied the law. Others had kept spiritual traditions alive by eliminating the features that government officials found most objectionable. But some spiritual ways had been lost forever.

Top Right:
Fine Day's headdress. Buffalo horn, ermine fur, human hair, glass beads, felt, muslin, feathers, canvas, brass, hide, cotton and metallic thread. Plains Cree. Early 1900s.

Despite government interference, the spiritual leader Fine Day fulfilled a vow he made as a young man to sponsor eight Sun Dances during his lifetime. He wore this headdress on the first day of dancing.

Above Right:
Healer's equipment. Hide, herbs, turquoise and cow horn. Cree. Early 1900s.

The pouch contains medicines used in treating headaches.

"My family lived right across the road [from the residential school]. But still, it was very odd, it was hard for me to understand why I couldn't just go home and go to school every day. I had to stay there. It was a very lonely time for me. I used to look outside and I could see my brothers and sisters playing outside. I used to cry. They were there, they were so close, and yet not close enough.

'It wasn't until maybe age 13 that I realized that all these kids [at the school] must have the same feelings. And some, their parents never came because they were away at work–you know, in the sugar beets, in the States, in B.C. I was lucky, more lucky than any of them. At least I saw them.

"When I think back, I have no regrets. Just that part that I was taken away from my parents. I learned a lot. And I'm who I am today because of what I learned."

Ann McMaster, Siksika.

Residential Schooling

When they signed treaties, Aboriginal leaders demanded that provisions be made for their children's education. They wanted future generations to have the skills to cope with a changing world.

The federal government saw schooling in a different light. As Prime Minister John A. Macdonald put it, "[T]he first object [of Indian education] is to make them better men, and if possible, good Christian men." This could best be achieved when children were removed from the "prejudicial influences" of home, family and community and placed in residential schools.

Ottawa turned to missionary orders and their existing network of mission schools to help implement its policy. The federal government would finance schools, and churches would staff and manage them.

Residential school curriculum featured the "four Rs"–reading, writing, arithmetic and religion. Class work was supplemented by a program of vocational training that had students spend half of each day working in school kitchens, barns and carpentry shops. When the Department of Indian Affairs cut back on school funding, children spent long hours stoking hay or sawing wood just to keep schools afloat.

Students' experiences at residential school varied. For some, attending residential school was a positive experience that taught

useful life skills. For others, the experience was devastating. Students often complained that discipline was too rigid and punishments severe. Most children experienced great loneliness. Some were abused.

Boarding schools for non-Aboriginal children shared some of these features. But the residential school experience was fundamentally different. Aboriginal children were removed from families and communities. Their identity was suppressed and their contact with their heritage curtailed. Overnight, they had to function in a totally different world.

Top:
St. Mary's School. Blood Reserve. Courtesy Provincial Archives of Alberta Oblate Collection OB 290.

Above Right:
Sewing-room at Dunbow Industrial School. Late 1800s. Courtesy Provincial Archives of Alberta Oblate Collection OB 8784.

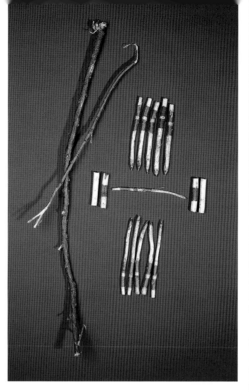

Quiet Resistance

Resistance to government policies rarely involved armed confrontation. It was more frequently expressed in formal protests, evasions and acts of non-compliance. This quiet resistance helped counter policies designed to assimilate Aboriginal people into Euro-Canadian society.

Many people resisted government policies by refusing to obey game restrictions. The treaties had guaranteed hunting and trapping rights, so they continued to camp in the forest, set controlled fires and hunt and trap as they had always done.

Residential schools inspired various acts of resistance. Some parents refused to let their children go. Others pushed for improved conditions by threatening to transfer their children to a school run by another church. Children took food from school kitchens, spoke their own language among themselves, and taught each other traditional songs and games. At St. Paul's Residential School on the Blood Reserve, students made their own hand game sets out of twigs they collected on the school grounds. When staff was not watching, older children showed younger ones how to play and taught them hand game songs.

People were particularly resolute in resisting attempts to suppress sacred ceremonies. In 1923, for instance, government and church authorities tried to stop a Sun Dance at Hobbema by arresting

Jacob Soosay, the man sponsoring the ceremony. They backed off when Chief Joe Samson intervened, saying that he would take Soosay's place in jail. The authorities were unwilling to imprison the influential Chief, and the Sun Dance proceeded unimpeded by outside interference.

Resistance also included finding new ways to express traditional values. At a time when sacred ceremonies were under government attack, communities across the northern Plains took up the Grass Dance. It likely originated with the Omaha or Pawnee First Nations in Nebraska. The Nakoda and Atsina introduced the Grass Dance to the Blackfoot and Tsuu T'ina in the 1880s. Originally a warrior society's dance, it became a secular powwow dance. The new dance brought people together in an affirmation of community solidarity and a celebration of survival during hard times. It emphasized that Aboriginal people had retained their distinctive cultural identity.

Top Left:
Roach . Porcupine and deer tail hair, hide and brass bell. Nakoda. Early 1900s.

Grass Dance dancers wear a special kind of headdress, known as a roach. The bristling movement it makes as a dancer moves evokes battling prairie chickens.

Top Right:
Hand game set. Wood. Kainai. 1997.

The hand game is a gambling game played at social gatherings. This set was made by Louis Soop, a former St. Paul's Residential School student, in the style of the improvised hand game sets used at St. Paul's.

Playing the Hand Game at School

"There's no real set rules on hand games. The way we used to play in the residential school is we'd sit in the corner, two players or more. You start with ten sticks. We used to have knives at school that we would use to whittle caragana trees [to make the hand game sticks], and then we'd put a design on some of the sticks. Then there are wooden bones that you use for hiding. You have two bones that you put in your hand. One has a wrap around the middle. You try to guess which one doesn't have that wrap. And every time that you can guess that, you take one of the sticks. It keeps on going until one side wins all ten sticks.

"Sometimes, we had people who knew how to sing hand game songs. They'd get a piece of stick and they'd just be drumming on the bench, on the floor, on anything. There's a certain beat for singing hand games; it's a real fast beat. The idea is to distract your opponent by singing these songs."

Louis Soop, Blood Tribe.

Destroying the Land

Government policies promoting resource development and private ownership of land spurred Alberta's economic growth during the early 20th century. These same policies, however, undermined traditional Aboriginal land use. Industrial expansion in particular had a devastating impact on Aboriginal economies. Forestry, hydro-development, mining, and oil and gas exploration all put tremendous pressure on resources. They also impeded access to hunting, trapping and fishing grounds.

> *"The white people said they were 'developing' the land. The old people called it 'destroying the land.' The 'development' caused the animals to move farther and farther away and we could no longer hunt in our traditional lands. The industries changed our lifestyles forever."*
>
> Francis Alexis, Nakoda, Alexis Band

Some communities responded to changing circumstances by organizing small-scale industrial ventures focused on local resource extraction. Sawmills provided an important source of income in the north, and several southern bands operated coalmines. While many of these initiatives were successful initially, they had difficulty competing over the long term with more heavily capitalized operations. In some instances, government-imposed restrictions hampered their activities. The Blackfoot Co-operative Coal Mine near Gleichen, for example, was prohibited from selling coal in towns that had their own mines. The mine closed in 1955, unable to compete with new, government-subsidized strip mines.

For many Aboriginal people, however, involvement in the industrial economy meant wage labour away from home. Jobs usually involved physical work or used skills based on knowledge of the land. Work was seasonal, sporadic and poorly paid. In southern Alberta, people found seasonal employment as farm labourers in the sugar beet fields. Sugar refineries and beet growers hired entire families, including young children, to thin plants, weed and hoe. In the north, where expanding transportation networks were key to industrial development, men cleared land for roadways, cut and hauled railway ties, and supplied wood for the fuel-burning sternwheelers that carried freight along the major rivers. Some people put their knowledge of the bush country to use working as road surveyors' guides. Others worked for farmers picking rocks, cutting tamarack and building fences.

> *"In the 1940s, there were lots of logging camps. People here skidded logs, worked in the sawmills, and piled and hauled lumber. Lots of the women worked as cooks in the logging camps. I used to cook for 250 men. They didn't treat me very well and called me 'squaw' but I kept my head high and did my work. I was there to help out my family."*
>
> Nancy Potts, Nakoda, Alexis Band

"For Every Three Families, One Plough and One Harrow"

(from Treaty Seven)

When treaties were signed, the federal government promised to help Indians develop new economies based on farming and ranching. Indians, for their part, were eager to learn to farm and ranch. The buffalo had disappeared, and they needed to build a new way of life. Some bands even surrendered some of their reserve lands to raise capital for their farms and ranches.

But Indians soon found that the government was not prepared to fund real agriculture. Treaty provisions of livestock, seed and farm implements proved inadequate, and families had to share basic equipment. On the Peigan reserve the band's lone tractor, binder and threshing machine were put into rotational use as people joined together to get major jobs done. Some farmers had to wait upwards of two months for a chance to use labour-saving equipment.

Heavy-handed supervision also worked to stifle economic initiative. Government-appointed farm instructors and Indian agents oversaw all operations. They made the crucial decisions about planting, harvesting and selling crops and livestock. Their decisions did not always serve the Indians' best interests.

In some instances, government policy prevented Indian farmers and ranchers from competing in the market economy. A "peasant farming" policy in effect from 1889 to 1897 was based on the notion that Indians had to experience subsistence farming before they could "progress" to a more advanced stage of production. They were not allowed to purchase labour-saving machinery and had to make their own tools. The insistence on inefficient methods and outmoded technology resulted in significant crop losses.

Other policies proved similarly counter-productive. An allotment policy implemented on some reserves assigned each family a small landholding of 40 acres at a time when white farmers were receiving 160 acres under the government's homestead policy. A permit system introduced in 1897 prohibited Indian farmers and ranchers from buying or selling produce or livestock without a permit from the Indian agent. Such close administration prevented farmers from exercising control over the products of their own labour.

Commercial farming became highly mechanized after World War II. Unable to raise capital or borrow money against reserve land, few Indian farmers could afford to buy the equipment needed for large-scale agricultural production. The land allotted them in any case was too small to support commercially viable farming operations. On some reserves, band members began leasing land to white farmers under an arrangement that saw much of the revenue derived from Indian lands leave the reserve. Only those reserves with substantial oil and gas deposits could afford the modern farming equipment necessary to compete with non-Aboriginal farmers.

"It seems like the Natives were pushed to farm. On the other hand, they were held back."

Elder Sophie Makinaw, Cree, Ermineskin Tribe.

Below:
Flail. Ash wood and leather. Plains Cree. Circa 1880. The Department of Indian Affairs' "peasant farming" policy, in effect from 1889 to 1897, meant that Indian farmers had to use hand-made tools at a time when white farmers were using steam-driven equipment.

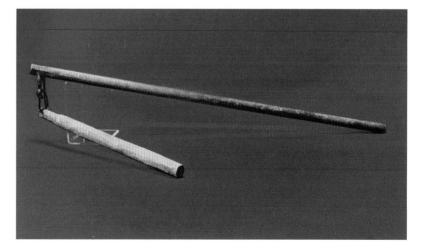

Inset Above:
Permit to sell a pony. Nakoda.
1937.

Right:
Tsuu T'ina cowboys branding cattle
in the early 1900s. Courtesy
Glenbow Archives NA-1437-8.

"Ranching Was the Biggest Thing"

"Ranching was the biggest thing on the reserve. We had our own band ranch. We used to run 2,000 head of band herd. . . If an individual couldn't feed his cow, the band would look after it and there was a fee. The whole layout was set up for the band, and everybody helped out."

Morris Little Wolf, Piikani.

Cattle ranching was introduced on southern Alberta reserves in the 1880s. It quickly proved more successful than farming. Not only was it better suited to the arid Plains environment, the work was more appealing. Ranching offered people the opportunity to parlay knowledge of the land and skill with animals into an enterprise that would support their families. Starting with small herds supplied by the federal government, reserve-based ranching operations steadily grew in size. By the mid-1900s, a number of families were engaged in successful ranching operations.

Several reserves operated band-owned ranches. Families grazed their herds on community pasturage, and men who did not themselves own livestock worked for the band ranch breaking horses, rounding up and branding cattle, repairing fences and cutting and hauling hay.

Bands sacrificed to make ranching work. Operations at Siksika, for example, were financed in large part by a trust fund established with proceeds from the sale of reserve lands. Agent George Gooderham used trust fund income to supply ranchers with livestock, wagons, barns and equipment. By 1940, ranching constituted the single largest source of income at Siksika. Its success, however, had come at considerable cost—Siksika land sales between 1911 and 1918 totalled close to 125,000 acres, or almost half the reserve.

As was the case with farming, government-imposed constraints hampered individual initiative. Ranchers couldn't sell or kill an animal without written permission from the Indian agent or farming instructor. The requirement that all sales be handled by the agency prevented ranchers from taking advantage of the higher prices offered by commercial beef handlers. The small-scale nature of reserve ranching also made it difficult to compete in an economic system increasingly dominated by corporate interests. Few Indian ranchers could afford steam ploughs, tractors or threshing machines, and individual land-holdings were too small to support large herds. Some people found it more profitable to lease grazing land to white ranchers than to try to raise cattle on an insufficient land base.

Despite these problems, cattle ranching offered an opportunity to build viable reserve-based economies. Along with such related enterprises as horse rearing and race horse training, it remains an important element of reserve life today.

Métis Settlements: Winning a Land Base

The Métis became increasingly marginalized in the years following Riel's Resistance and the disastrous scrip program. Many became road allowance people. They lived on strips of Crown land alongside roads or on the outskirts of towns and supported themselves with wage labour and by hunting and trapping.

Times grew tougher with the onset of the Depression. Then, in 1930, responsibility for natural resources was transferred from Ottawa to the provinces. New provincial game laws were passed restricting access to hunting and trapping areas. Lands on which the road allowance people had been squatting were slated for resource development. People would be evicted from their homes.

This latest threat sparked the Métis re-emergence as a political force. In 1932 a new political organization, l'Association des Métis d'Alberta, was formed. Its sustained pressure on the provincial government led to passage of the Métis Population Betterment Act of 1938. Under the Act, Alberta set aside twelve parcels of Crown land as farming colonies, or settlements, and promised funding for economic development and health programs. Eight of the 12 original settlements still exist. They are located in north-central Alberta and encompass 1.25 million acres. In 1995, they were home to about 5000 of Alberta's 60,000 Métis.

There were drawbacks. Government-appointed supervisors oversaw settlement activities. Settlement locations were remote, good-paying jobs were hard to come by, and much of the land was unsuitable for farming. And, while settlement land was reserved for Métis use, another 50 years would pass before they gained legal title. But the Métis had come together as an organized political force. The road allowance people had a place to call home.

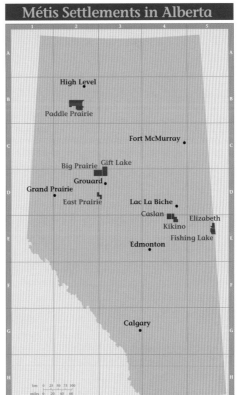

Métis Settlements in Alberta

Above:
"The Big Five": Executive Committee of L'Association des Métis d'Alberta (known today as the Métis Nation of Alberta Association). 1935. Courtesy Glenbow Archives.

Back, L to R: Peter Tomkins, Felix Calihoo. Front, L to R: Malcolm Norris, Joseph Dion, James Brady.

Right:
Alberta is unique among Canadian provinces in having set aside lands for the Métis.

Unknown Soldiers

"When we came out, we were supposed to get waiting benefits. That's for waiting until you can establish yourself. Waiting benefits and out of work benefits. We didn't get all of those. That's what we're still fighting for since '45 . . . You know, there is always a big fuss in the First World War and then this one about the Unknown Soldier. How about us? There were thousands and thousands of Aboriginal soldiers that returned. They're all Unknown Soldiers."

Mark Wolf Leg, Sr. Siksika.

Defending Canada Abroad, Fighting for Justice at Home

Over 12,000 First Nations, Métis and Inuit people fought for Canada in the First and Second World Wars and in Korea. Their enlistment rate–35 percent of those eligible–was the highest among all ethnic and cultural groups in Canada. Aboriginal soldiers were represented in every rank of the service, from Private to Brigadier, and won numerous medals and commendations.

Thousands more showed their support on the home front. Aboriginal farmers stepped up production. Women organized Red Cross societies and knitted socks and sweaters for soldiers in the trenches. Bands purchased war savings certificates and donated a portion of their annual treaty payments to the national treasury.

These contributions seldom won the recognition they deserved. Under the War Measures Act, under-developed reserve lands were leased to non-Aboriginal farmers to boost agricultural production. Much of this land was subsequently surrendered under the Soldier Settlement Act of 1919 to provide non-Aboriginal veterans with homesteads. Aboriginal soldiers returning from the Second World War missed out on veterans' home improvement grants and educational opportunities enjoyed by other veterans. When they tried to collect on benefits, they were shuttled back and forth between the Departments of Veterans' Affairs and Indian Affairs. Neither department would accept responsibility for administering the benefits to which these veterans were entitled.

Veterans often returned home with a new political awareness. They had witnessed first-hand the consequences of racial hatred; they had laid down their lives in defense of human rights halfway around the world. They returned to Canada determined to continue the struggle for rights at home. Now, they would fight for their own people.

Above:
Corporal Robert J. Berard, Métis, lays a wreath for Aboriginal veterans at the Remembrance Ceremony marking the 50th anniversary of the liberation of the Netherlands in World War II by Canadian armed forces. Groesbeek Canadian War Cemetery, May 6, 1995. Courtesy Robert Berard.

Left:
Kainai and Siksika recruits in the 191st Battalion. Fort MacLeod, 1916. Courtesy Glenbow Institute NA-2164-1.

Loss and Survival

The post-war years brought prosperity to much of Canada. Indian reserves and Métis settlements, however, remained underdeveloped. Many Aboriginal people lived in one or two-room mud shacks with floors of hardened mud or wood boards. Few communities had electricity or running water.

Aboriginal communities faced a number of other barriers to development. The Indian Act and the discriminatory laws that it had spawned sharply restricted political expression. Indians were prohibited from organizing politically, and those who lived on reserves could not vote in federal or provincial elections. They were not allowed to own land or businesses on reserves, nor could they borrow money from lending institutions. Status Indians were denied funding for post-secondary education and seldom had the resources to finance their own education. Aboriginal people had become second-class citizens in a country that had once been theirs.

The sustained assault on culture and beliefs had created personal and social problems. Many people suffered lack of pride, alcoholism and family breakdown. Frequent encounters with social welfare agencies and the penal system had devastating long-term effects. Prejudice reinforced this harsh reality, as some individuals came to feel that they had to deny their Aboriginal identity if they were to succeed in the outside world.

The postwar years, however, were also a time of growing international awareness of human rights issues. Under the leadership of Prime Minister John Diefenbaker, the Indian Act was revised to permit cultural and political expression. The amended versions of the Indian Act enacted in 1951 and 1960 reduced the degree of government intrusion into Aboriginal peoples' lives and extended basic democratic rights that had been previously denied. These changes opened the door to participation in Canadian society.

The revised Indian Act did not differ in its overall outlook from earlier legislation; assimilation remained its primary aim. But it did eliminate some discriminatory provisions. The Indian Act of 1951 rescinded prohibitions on traditional spiritual practices, lifted a ban on political organizing and granted Indians freedom of movement and association. The Indian Act of 1960 extended the right to vote in federal elections. The right to vote in provincial elections came in 1965 with the revision of Alberta's Elections Act.

These changes in government policy were important. They allowed Aboriginal people to organize politically, express their discontent and voice their desire for self-determination. The underlying poverty that haunted so many communities, however, remained largely unaddressed.

Tuberculosis and the Hospitalization Experience

Mortality rates from tuberculosis reached epidemic proportions in Aboriginal communities during the 1930s. In response, the federal government began evacuating people with active tuberculosis from their home communities and institutionalizing them in hospitals located in major population centres. Segregating individuals with this highly contagious disease in facilities offering specialized treatment reduced the number of new cases, but there were heavy personal and social costs. Prolonged hospitalization had lasting effects on people's lives. Patients were separated from their spouses, families and

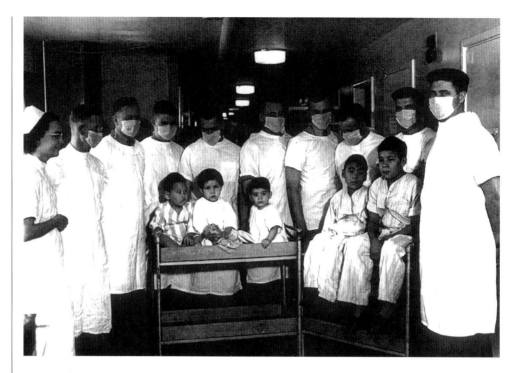

communities for years at a time. Children often lost their cultural identity and could not adjust once they returned home.

The Charles Camsell Indian Hospital in Edmonton was the largest centre in Canada devoted to treating Aboriginal people with tuberculosis. Established in 1945, it became home for many Aboriginal people from Alberta and the Northwest Territories. Staff at the Charles Camsell encouraged patients to speak their own language and to create art and craft objects. They provided connections to home communities through a radio program that broadcast messages from patients to family and friends back home.

Still, the hospital environment and strict routine were far removed from patients' lifestyles and cultures. And in the patients' home communities, the long absence of family members frequently created economic difficulties and increased family and social problems.

"I was about four when my father went into the hospital for tuberculosis. Every time he came home, he was a stranger to me, a different person. I never really knew him. It was hard. It affected my mother and family so much."

Elizabeth Roberts, Inuit, Resolute Bay.

Protest and Struggle

In the late 1960s and 1970s, new political leaders emerged in the Aboriginal community. They spoke out against the sub-standard living conditions many Aboriginal people faced and organized grassroots movements to work for social change.

Influenced by social activism and civil rights movements in other parts of the world, the new generation of Aboriginal political leaders challenged the social and economic problems they saw in their communities. They organized rallies, held protest marches, conducted investigations into living conditions on reserves and settlements and demanded to be included in the development of government Aboriginal policies.

"Fox Lake Investigation" postcard. 1966.

The Fox Lake Investigation

Two of the most prominent forces for change in the post-war years were the Indian Association of Alberta (IAA) and the Métis Association of Alberta (MAA). These organizations began by focusing on bread and butter issues. One of their best-known actions took place in the fall of 1966, when the Department of Indian Affairs and Northern Development hired IAA president John Samson and Alberta Native Federation fieldworker Stan Daniels to investigate living conditions in Fox Lake, a small Cree community in northern Alberta.

Their findings were explosive. Fox Lake residents lived in small, crowded buildings without running water, electricity or reliable heating. Most houses were in disrepair, and food supplies were inadequate. To make matters worse, the Hudson's Bay Company store exploited its position as the only store in town to charge inflated prices on basic goods. Beef sausage selling for 78 cents per pound at the time in Edmonton, for example, was priced at $2.98 per pound at the Company store. Many Fox Lake residents signed over their entire monthly cheques to the store to cover outstanding charges.

When the Department of Indian Affairs failed to respond to their report, Samson and Daniels hitchhiked across the country to take their findings directly to Prime Minister Lester Pearson. Armed with a homemade poster reading "Sausage for the P.M." and a bill of sale from the Fox Lake store for a pound of sausage, they set out from Edmonton on November 7, 1966. When they arrived in Ottawa a week later, Pearson asked them to meet with Minister of Indian Affairs Otto Laing. The Minister, however, refused their request to allow Harold Cardinal, at that time president of the National Indian Youth Council, to join the meeting, and Samson and Daniels returned home. While they had failed to present their case to the government, they had succeeded in drawing media coverage of the deplorable state of affairs in Alberta's northern communities.

The White and Red Papers

The 1960s also marked the emergence of First Nations nationalism as a force in Canadian politics. The spark was lit in 1969, when the newly elected Liberal government of Pierre Trudeau introduced its White Paper on Indian Policy. The policy statement was overwhelmingly rejected by Aboriginal people and became a stimulus for First Nations activism.

The White Paper, sweeping in scope and dramatic in impact, was the capstone of government assimilation policy. With its proposals to repeal the Indian Act and renounce the Treaties, it advocated the abolition of all federal responsibilities towards First Nations and termination of their special constitutional status.

Aboriginal people across the country rejected the initiative. The Indian Chiefs of Alberta took the lead role in opposing the Trudeau plan with publication of their Citizens Plus document, popularly known as the Red Paper. The Red Paper, which advocated reaffirmation of Indians' special status and full recognition of Treaty rights, became the official national Indian response.

Further opposition came from Harold Cardinal, president of the Indian Association of Alberta from 1968 to 1977. His book, *The Unjust Society*, attacked the White Paper as "a thinly disguised program of extermination through assimilation." Cardinal argued that Indians should be empowered to manage their own affairs and shape their own destinies. He also insisted that they should enjoy the rights guaranteed them under Treaties. These included the right to medical care, the right to post-secondary education, the right to hunt, fish and trap, and the right to land.

In 1970, Cardinal and National Indian Brotherhood president George Manuel led a delegation to Ottawa that met with Trudeau and his Indian Affairs Minister, Jean Chrétien. The delegation's unequivocal

The IAA and the Red Paper

"With the tabling of the '69 White Paper, once we [the Indian Association of Alberta] were sure that we understood what was being proposed, we shifted our energies to going from community to community to explain the contents of that Paper. And we began the process of developing a counterproposal because it was unacceptable to us and we weren't satisfied with just saying no. I think we took a year to develop a counterproposal which subsequently became known as the Red Paper; the official title was Citizens Plus. That was the product of a year of intense community, regional, and provincial meetings. I don't know how many drafts and redrafts we went through because we had to go word by word, line by line, with all the people in all the communities. We had to translate it from many different languages to make sure that it reflected what the people were saying.

"[W]hen we were ready, our Chiefs went from Alberta, an extremely large delegation, to table our proposal and to try to garner national support for the document, which we succeeded in getting. We also succeeded, and I think for us this was probably the major breakthrough, in securing a meeting with the Prime Minister and members of his cabinet. In fact, that was probably one of the first times that the Prime Minister sat down to those substantive discussions. I think other than that they were photo ops. So we were able to make the presentation and we had a commitment from the late Prime Minister Trudeau to put the White Paper on hold and get the dialogue going."

Harold Cardinal, Sucker Creek Band.

rejection of the White Paper led to its retraction in 1971 and the adoption of a new approach to developing Indian policy. Until then, federal Indian policy had been developed with little input from First Nations. Now, First Nations would be consulted on issues that affected them.

Addressing Urban Needs

During the 1960s and 1970s, many Aboriginal people moved from reserves and settlements to urban areas. Facing unemployment, poverty and crowded conditions at home, some people saw relocation to cities as the best chance to improve their quality of life. Cities offered access to higher education and greater employment opportunities than were available on reserves or settlements. The Department of Indian Affairs encouraged the movement to urban areas by offering housing grants. The transition from rural to urban life, however, was not always easy. Cultural and linguistic barriers, discrimination, and the absence of family and community support often made the adjustment to this new way of life difficult.

A number of organizations were established to provide support services for urban Aboriginal residents. One of the most influential was the network of Native Friendship Centres. Alberta's first Centre opened in Edmonton in 1962. Friendship Centres initially served as drop-in centres where people could socialize with one another. Some provided referral services and individual counseling. They later expanded their services to include Aboriginal language programs, arts and crafts instruction, dances, talent contests and sporting events. The Centres helped ease the transition from rural to urban life and provided the impetus for the formation of other service organizations and community groups.

The Healing Movement

In the early 1970s, Aboriginal people began to address the pain and turmoil they saw in their communities. They resolved to overcome the social problems that were the legacy of the past one hundred years through treatment and healing. Building on the efforts of leaders and activists, people began reclaiming pride in their culture and identity. Traditional spiritual values re-emerged under the guidance of Elders, traditionalists and "keepers of the ways". Many of these values were incorporated into healing processes.

The healing movement's initial focus was on alcoholism, but it soon expanded to address the social factors underlying addictions, including sexual abuse, domestic violence, suicide and the loss of cultural and spiritual identity. Eric Shirt of Saddle Lake established one of the most influential healing facilities in Edmonton in 1973. Poundmaker's Lodge, named after Chief Poundmaker, an outspoken critic of alcohol use, offers counseling, educational workshops and a supportive environment for personal growth. It was the first addictions treatment centre operated by Aboriginal people in Canada. A sister institution, the Nechi Institute, opened in 1974. It provides addictions counsellor training and community education programs.

Aboriginal people continue to address issues of addiction and dysfunction through culturally unique approaches. They include Elders' counselling, healing circles, sentencing circles, and wilderness living camps. Underlying all these approaches is the belief that spiritual healing is as important as physical healing.

Below:
Counselling session at Poundmaker's Lodge Outpatients' Clinic. 1980. Courtesy Provincial Archives of Alberta J.4861/6.

Spiritual Revitalization

Despite the best efforts of church and state, traditional spirituality and teachings did not disappear during the years of assimilationist policy. Even during the darkest days of government interference with spiritual practices, people continued to follow traditional spiritual teachings. Often, they did so in secret. Following the 1951 amendments to the Indian Act, however, traditional ceremonies could be conducted without fear of reprisals. Elders and traditionalists who had kept sacred knowledge alive were sought out by new generations.

Today, people of all ages recognize the dignity and strength of traditional ceremonies and practice them openly. Sun Dances and Thunder Medicine Pipe ceremonies are held on many Alberta reserves, and some sacred societies have been revived. Through the Pan-Indian movement, some people also have incorporated practices and beliefs originating with other First Nations.

Some Aboriginal people also express spirituality through Christian prayer. In an effort to reach out to Aboriginal parishioners, some Christian services incorporate traditional spiritual practices. Sweetgrass may be burned in place of incense, for example, and prayers and hymns are offered in Aboriginal languages.

"The teachings that were handed down to me on pipe making show that the traditional ways have been ongoing. We have lost some, but the teachings that are still in existence have come from the Elders."

Jerry Potts, Jr.

Reclaiming Voice: Contemporary Initiatives

Over the past few decades, First Nations and Métis communities have taken increasing control over the administration of social services. Locally controlled initiatives in the areas of economic development, health, education, child welfare and justice provide the opportunity to shape policy in culturally sensitive ways that address community-identified needs. These gains have been hard-won; each step forward has come about as the result of sustained political pressure.

Much remains to be done. Aboriginal people remain the poorest segment of the Canadian population. Infant mortality is twice the national average, and life expectancy is significantly lower than that of other Canadian citizens. The majority of Aboriginal youth do not finish high school, and the percentage of children in the child welfare system is roughly four times greater for Aboriginal than non-Aboriginal populations. Aboriginal communities are approaching these challenges with determination and a renewed sense of self-reliance.

Self-Government

Aboriginal people are redefining political relations with federal and provincial governments. These efforts are opening the door to regaining control over their affairs.

Alberta First Nations have successfully negotiated settlements of outstanding land claims with the federal government. They also have secured increasing responsibility for administering a wide range of social and economic programs in their communities. Today, First Nations operate most on-reserve services – from health, education and welfare programs to infrastructure development.

The special relationship between Alberta Métis and the provincial government likewise has continued to evolve. In 1990, the Alberta Federation of Métis Settlements and the Government of Alberta signed an agreement confirming the grant of Settlement lands to the Métis Settlements General Council on a permanent basis. Other provisions granted limited self-government, partial control over oil and gas development, funds for capital improvements and a trust fund of about $140,000,000. The Métis Nation of Alberta Association, meanwhile, developed a 1987 Framework Agreement with the Alberta government that promotes economic development, social and education programs, and environmental protection services for off-Settlement Métis. Whatever shape self-government takes, most Aboriginal people agree that sovereignty and a secure land base are key to their communities' future well being.

Economic Development

The struggle for economic sufficiency has been long and painful. Indian Act prohibitions on using reserve land or resources as collateral discourage conventional lending institutions from lending to reserve-based enterprises. Lack of capital, limited educational opportunities and a dearth of jobs in their home communities have further hampered Aboriginal peoples' efforts to achieve economic development.

Peace Hills Trust, a chartered financial trust company owned by the Samson Cree Nation at Hobbema, was established in part to address the unique financial circumstances facing Aboriginal communities. The company, chartered in 1981, finances infrastructure development and assists Aboriginal entrepreneurs in communities across Canada. While this

Above:
Bottles of "Spirit Water" and pamphlets. Cree. 1997.

The Sawridge Band in Slave Lake owns several hotels, a truck stop, an apartment complex and a shopping mall. The band-owned Spirit Water Company was founded in 1993 and owns rights to a glacier in British Columbia.

Right:
The first graduates of the Indigenous Law Program at the University of Alberta. 1994. Left to right: Troy Chalifoux, Bradley Enge, Brian Wigger, Caroline Buffalo and Art Tralenberg. Missing: Christopher Lafleur. Courtesy Bradley Enge.

Some communities have established partnerships with corporations. Corporate partners typically contribute capital, management and marketing expertise, while communities offer workers, land-based resources and tax advantages. Joint venture enterprises organized along these lines include logging operations, oil and gas exploration, pipeline construction and other resource extraction activities.

innovative banking institution serves both Aboriginal and non-Aboriginal clients, it has a special mandate to service First Nations communities. Peace Hills Trust has developed a culturally sensitive approach to Aboriginal business people's need and offers a full range of financial services, including loans, mortgages, asset and investment management, and retirement savings plans.

Recent land claims settlements and court decisions enabling First Nations and Métis Settlements to develop local resources have encouraged some economic growth. They've also made it possible to develop long-term business plans and to amass capital for investment in community-owned enterprises. These enterprises, which range from gas bars and oil-well servicing ventures to country clubs and fly-in fishing lodges, bring in much-needed jobs and income.

In addition to these cooperative efforts, many individuals and community organizations have established independent businesses, often building on established arts or crafts traditions. Aboriginal entrepreneurs, however, can be found in any field of enterprise.

Education

In 1972, the National Indian Brotherhood issued a landmark education policy paper. It stated that First Nations parents must have full responsibility for their children's education and that bands must be invested with the authority for education on reserves.

The federal government agreed to these proposals and in 1973 implemented a new policy that gradually transferred control over on-reserve schools to bands. In 1974, over forty federally operated schools existed on Alberta reserves. Today, all but one of the province's First Nations exercise control over their own schools.

Progress also has occurred at the post-secondary level. Locally controlled First Nations colleges such as Blue Quills College at Saddle Lake, Maskwachees Cultural College at Hobbema, and Red Crow College on the Blood Reserve provide students with the opportunity to further their education while keeping in touch with their culture and community. Staff members often are from the local community and provide positive role models. In urban areas, major provincial institutions such as the University of Alberta and the University of Lethbridge offer degrees in Native Studies and Native Education. Universities also offer support services for Aboriginal students. The Indigenous Law Program at the University of Alberta, for example, offers Aboriginal law students academic, career and employment counseling. Programs such as these aim to redress the under-representation of Aboriginal people in Canada's professional ranks and to bring Aboriginal perspectives and interests to bear in a variety of fields.

Amiskwaciy Academy

In the early 1990s, Edmonton's Aboriginal community began working with Edmonton Public Schools to create a high school that would meet Aboriginal students' needs. Dr. Phyllis Cardinal set up community meetings to discuss the shape the school should take. Elders and community members shared ideas regarding the school's vision, its academic curriculum and its architectural design. Amiskwaciy Academy opened in September 2000 with an enrolment of approximately 240 students. Enrolment had increased to 350 by 2003.

Amiskwaciy is a university preparatory school that operates within the framework of the Edmonton Public Schools. It offers all the courses required by Alberta Learning while providing an Aboriginal perspective. Students take Aboriginal Studies classes and have the option of studying Cree language and traditional dance. Students participate in meditation, sweetgrass ceremonies and smudging. An Elders-in-Residence program provides an opportunity for Elders to share their knowledge of Aboriginal culture with students, and teams of Elders, parents, teachers and counselors are on hand for guidance.

"They [the teachers] really make us feel good about ourselves, and they always tell us that no matter what, you have the potential to succeed. Just as long as you put your mind to it, you can do it. And, you know, if people tell you that all the time, you really do start to believe it. And that's what Amiskwaciy does. I'm really happy to have that in my life. I'm really grateful.

"My personal goals are to become a dentist. I've never seen an Aboriginal dentist before, so I kind of want to see what it would be like. I know that, not so much for the money or the work, it's just that I know that I could do something. I know that it would leave an impression on Aboriginal patients and even the non-Aboriginal patients–because, 'wow, look at that, somebody went somewhere in their life!'"

Natashia Cardinal, Amiskwaciy Academy student.

Health Care

The state of health in many Aboriginal communities is poor. A 1999 World Health Organization report found that Aboriginal Canadians have substantially higher rates of tuberculosis, diabetes, suicide, violent death and alcohol-related illness and injury than any other segment of the population. Aboriginal people are addressing these problems by becoming actively involved in providing culturally sensitive health care services.

In 1987, the federal government began transferring to Aboriginal communities the authority to plan and deliver health services. With transferred authority came greater flexibility in the use of funds, greater freedom to adapt services to local needs, and a sense of community ownership of health service facilities and programs.

The health transfer policy's limited scope, however, has prevented communities from developing comprehensive health care systems. Access to health services remains limited in most reserve communities, while off-reserve facilities present formidable linguistic and cultural barriers to many Aboriginal patients. Still, increased numbers of trained Aboriginal health care

professionals and the development of culturally appropriate support services are making inroads towards improving health care. Aboriginal representatives on provincial Regional Health Authority boards help ensure that Aboriginal concerns are considered in policy development, and initiatives such as the Capital Health Aboriginal Wellness program in Edmonton provide patients and families in urban hospitals with interpretive services and culturally sensitive support.

Justice and Policing

By the early 1960s approximately 60 percent of people in the Alberta criminal justice system were Aboriginal. Many of these individuals faced problems of linguistic and cultural difference, and most were unfamiliar with court proceedings. Aboriginal organizations began working to secure better treatment for Aboriginal people.

The first step forward was made when Chester Cunningham, a court worker with the Canadian Native Friendship Centre in Edmonton, began providing services to assist Aboriginal people appearing in court. He interpreted, explained court procedures and provided counseling. The Métis and Indian Associations of Alberta, in co-operation with the provincial government, expanded those services when they established a province-wide Aboriginal court worker program in 1970. It was administered through Native Counselling Services, a private, non-profit organization formed that same year.

Continuing pressure from the Métis and Indian Associations pushed the provincial government to hold enquiries into Aboriginal concerns with the justice system. Province-wide commissions launched in 1973 and 1990 recommended more Aboriginal input into all aspects of justice administration. As a result, Aboriginal people today operate on-reserve correctional facilities and pursue community-based initiatives such as sentencing circles, youth justice committees and wilderness camps offering offenders job skills training and spiritual guidance from Elders.

An initiative launched in the fall of 1999 saw the first Aboriginal court in Canada established on the Tsuu T'ina First Nation. Presided over by Provincial Court Judge Tony Mandamin, the court hears criminal, civil, family and youth matters involving Aboriginal defendants. It emphasizes healing over punishment and makes Aboriginal practices such as sentencing circles part of dispute resolution and sentencing.

Efforts to make the justice system responsive to Aboriginal concerns also have emphasized increased Aboriginal involvement in policing. The RCMP's Native Policing Program, inaugurated in 1974, offered Aboriginal Special Constables increased levels of training and responsibility. A conversion program initiated in the early 1990s eliminated the Special Constable status and upgraded all eligible members to Regular Constable status. By 1996, there were 68 Aboriginal RCMP officers working in Alberta.

The Arts

Traditional First Nations societies did not distinguish between the sacred and the secular. Art and creativity were intrinsically expressed in all aspects of life. Everyday functional items, such as clothing and tipis, were created to reflect and honour the spiritual.

Contemporary artists use traditional art forms, modern art forms, or a combination of the two. Some adapt media and technology to provide insightful perspectives on Aboriginal experiences. Many Aboriginal artists from Alberta have won prestigious awards and gained national and international acclaim.

Although Aboriginal artists use various media and genres, their work often is grounded in a strong spiritual awareness. Artists express confidence and pride in their identity. Art has become a powerful medium for expressing Aboriginal vision and voice.

Above:
Papamihaw Asini-Flying Rock. Stewart Steinhauer. Cree. Brazilian soapstone. 1999.

This sculpture was inspired by the Manitou Stone displayed in the Gallery.

"The big buffalo represents the as-yet-unknowable origins of life, the universe and everything. The small buffalo represents the pre-colonial Cree economy and is an abstract symbol for a possible future viable economy. Inside the big buffalo there is a representation of a sweatlodge. Two Elders sit inside, shaking rattles and singing. Papamihaw Asini, the Flying Rock, is in the sky above them. Even though 133 years have passed since the Flying Rock was taken prisoner, the song that the Elders sing contains his memory. Each generation learns the song and keeps his memory alive. A channel runs from the sweatlodge to the big buffalo's eyes. In this manner, past and future are connected by visionary feeling, thought and action".

Stewart Steinhauer